Social Justice:

The Teachings of Catholics, Protestants, Jews, and Muslims

*With Special Emphasis on the American
Catholic Bishops' Pastoral Letters on Peace and War,
on the Economy, and on the Concerns of Women*

James J. Horgan   Lucy Fuchs

Editors

Jeanine Jacob   Jude Michael Ryan
Bernard S. Parker   Christine Cherry Cernik
Joseph A. Cernik   David T. Borton
S. Mary David Hydro, O.S.B.   Kathleen Kosuda
Charles Lewis Fisk Jr.   John J. McTague

Saint Leo College Press
Saint Leo, Florida
1992

Cover: Woodcut (1963) by Irving Amen.
           Used by permission of the artist.

Excerpts from the Catholic Bishops' pastoral letters *The Challenge of Peace* (1983) and *Economic Justice for All* (1986), and the draft pastoral *Partners in the Mystery of Redemption* (1988) used by permission of the National Conference of Catholic Bishops.

Library of Congress Catalog Card Number 92-081090
ISBN 0-945759-04-5
Printed in the United States of America

Published by
Saint Leo College Press
P. O. Box 2247
Saint Leo, Florida 33574

Table of Contents

Introduction

This is a book about how people should treat one another. More specifically, it examines the social teachings of four major religions: Catholicism, Protestantism, Judaism, and Islam.

In the opening chapter, James J. Horgan examines the social teaching of the Catholic Church. Despite its long tradition, this church has been promulgating a formal body of social teaching only since Pope Leo XIII's 1891 encyclical letter "On the Condition of Working People." Subsequent social encyclicals, as well as the documents of the Second Vatican Council (1962-1965) and the statements of bishops' conferences, carried the teaching further. Its underlying principle is human dignity. In the past century, the Catholic Church has shifted from an emphasis on charity to a focus on justice and from a posture of support for the status quo to the encouragement of social change.

We emphasize the three statements the American Catholic Bishops have issued in recent years on issues of social justice: their pastoral letters *The Challenge of Peace* (1983) and *Economic Justice for All* (1986), as well as the first published draft of their proposed pastoral on the concerns of women, entitled *Partners in the Mystery of Redemption* (1988). Excerpts of each statement, composed by Jeanine Jacob, are presented at the beginning of each two-chapter commentary on the letters.

Bernard S. Parker analyzes the philosophical underpinnings of the Catholic Bishops' pastoral on issues of peace and war. He explains the traditional criteria for a "just war" — just cause, competent authority, comparative justice, right intention, last resort, probability of success, proportionality — and then examines the bishops's commentary on the policy of nuclear deterrence. They condemn the use of nuclear weapons, but at the same time they accept the concept of deterrence. The bishops recognize that the "paradox" of this position strains their "moral conception." "May a nation threaten what it may never do?" they write. "May it possess what it may never use?"

A different perspective on the war-and-peace pastoral is taken by Joseph A. Cernik. He discusses "The Catholic Bishops as Political Activists" by exploring the national political climate in which the pastoral was written: arms control negotiations, the nuclear freeze movement, and the increased military budget of the administration of Ronald Reagan. He goes on to analyze the reaction to the letter from all parts of the political spectrum. The bishops tried to be detached from partisanship in issuing their moral guidelines, and they were deliberately ambiguous in some of their judgments. Despite these efforts, their foray into public policy brought them much criticism.

S. Mary David Hydro, O.S.B. presents an analysis of the Catholic Bishops' pastoral letter on economic justice. She reviews the document and focuses on four problems and the bishops' suggested solutions: a national commitment to provide full employment, a concerted effort to eradicate poverty, a legislative program to protect family farms, and an international mobilization to assist other nations economically. Their vision for social justice flows from this central principle: "Every economic decision and institution must be judged in light of whether it protects or undermines the dignity of the human person."

Charles L. Fisk analyzes the practicality of the Catholic Bishops' pastoral letter *Economic Justice for All.* Can these moral principles be achieved in a capitalist economy? He provides an explanation of basic economic concepts, including the drive for profit at the core of capitalism, and finds the moral question of justice in conflict with the nature of this economic system. The issues of full employment, just wages, and provision for the human needs of housing and medical care must be addressed in the political arena, for they cannot be solved by the marketplace alone.

Jude Ryan examines the substance of the first published draft of the Catholic Bishops' 1988 proposed pastoral letter on the concerns of women. The bishops for the first time explicitly categorize sexism as "sin" and call for society to recognize and respond to the needs of women as human beings. Furthermore, they acknowledge the failings of the Church itself in being consistently sensitive to these concerns. "The great accomplishment of the American Bishops' letter," he writes, "may reside in its creators' willingness to engage in controversial debates by raising questions about issues on which there is no absolute consensus."

In her chapter on the same pastoral draft, Christine Cherry Cernik reviews the history of "Catholic feminism" and the genesis of the bishops' statement. She outlines the document, cites its central points, and discusses reactions from a range of commentators. This first published draft on the concerns of women drew more criticism than the bishops' two earlier pastorals on war and peace and on economic justice. Some traditionalists took the view that the bishops were going too far; some progressives argued that they had not gone far enough. The issue remains "unfinished business."

Lucy Fuchs surveys the actions which have taken place to implement the Catholic Bishops' statements on all three of these pastoral topics. In the case of the peace pastoral, she finds that while its impact on parishioners in the pew has been uneven, the letter did contribute to the societal debate on the utility of war. With their statement on the economy, the bishops had greater effect by establishing and funding a formal program to carry out their vision for economic justice. On the concerns of women, the bishops are still struggling to develop their final thinking. "What is especially significant," she concludes, "is the wide consultation and serious study the bishops have promoted on issues that concern the entire human family."

In "Protestant Social Teaching," David T. Borton examines general aspects of the Protestant approach to social policy and then focuses on three denominations as illustrations: the Presbyterian Church (USA), the Episcopal Church, and the United Methodist Church. Unlike other denominations which emphasize an individual's personal relationship with God, these three branches of Protestantism have each articulated distinct positions on social issues. He explores three areas in particular: war and peace, economics, and the concerns of women — the same ones examined by the American Catholic Bishops. He concludes that "this pilgrim church must continue to find its way 'to do justly, and to love mercy, and to walk humbly' with God."

The social teachings of Judaism are explored by Kathleen Kosuda, who quotes an ancient rabbi on the essence of its religious message: "That which is hateful to you, do not do to your neighbor. This is the entire Torah. . . ." She discusses the sources of Jewish thought and the nature of the Jewish tradition and then reviews the positions of Judaism on economic justice, on peace and war, and on women. "Judaism is an ethical system as well as a formal religion concerned with human behavior," she notes. "Its fundamental principle of the Golden Rule is a guideline of timeless value."

Of all the religions examined here, Islam is the least familiar to Americans. John J. McTague finds that Islam has much in common with Judaism and Christianity. He examines its origins; analyzes the distinctions in its major sects, the Sunnis and the Shi'ites; and explains the Five Pillars, which outline the basic duties of all Muslims. In his exploration of social teaching, he concludes that in two areas — economics and war-and-peace issues — Islam is similar to the Judeo-Christian tradition; on the status of women, however, Islam has not experienced the same currents influencing other Western religions.

It is not our purpose to present a comprehensive analysis of the social teachings of every religion. We hope that our exploration of those we examine here will provide greater understanding of these issues.

We thank in particular Jeanne M. Sundberg and Barbara A. Berger for their technical assistance with this book.

James J. Horgan
Saint Leo, Florida
May 1992

James J. Horgan

The Social Teaching of the Catholic Church

"If you want peace, work for justice," said Pope Paul VI in 1972.[1] Simply put, this statement captures the spirit in which the Catholic Church endorses personal responsiveness in the development of a just society.

The international College of Bishops meeting in Rome in 1971 took a similarly forceful position in its document *Justice in the World*, which for the first time overtly characterized the pursuit of social justice on earth as central to the mission of the Catholic Church.

> Action on behalf of justice and participation in the transformation of the world fully appear to us as a constitutive dimension of the preaching of the Gospel, or, in other words, of the Church's mission for the redemption of the human race and its liberation from every oppressive situation.[2]

Such a broad advocacy of social change and earthly liberation in the name of justice may seem surprising for a church whose long-time image projected a conservative, hierarchical organization, noteworthy for its defense of the status quo, its battles for dogmatic orthodoxy, and its focus on things of the spirit as the path to salvation.

In this regard, a 1987 monograph on Catholic social teaching was bluntly entitled *Our Best Kept Secret*, and the authors took note of what they considered a lamentable situation: "*That* the church has a developed body of social teaching on social, economic, political and cultural matters and *what* that body says seems to have been forgotten — or never known — by a majority of the Roman Catholic community in this country."[3]

Many Catholics are not only unaware of their church's teaching on social justice, they even reject its involvement in such temporal matters as inappropriate. This sentiment was reflected in a 1986 interview in the *New Catholic World* with the board chairman of an investment firm. He was critical of the just-published American Bishops' pastoral letter on the economy:

> The Church should do what it does best — providing for the spiritual lives of people; being there for the sick, the dying, the troubled; helping people when they are in need. But they shouldn't be making big universal statements on the economy! Economic thought is very complex. Businessmen just do not see the Church as part of this field. . . . the bishops are in over their heads on this.[4]

Despite such reactions, the American Bishops — not only in their pastoral letter on the economy, but also in those on peace and war and on women — were not dabbling in novelty. They were carrying forward a well established tradition of the Catholic Church and acting from a broad body of social doctrine.

Sources of Catholic Social Teaching

The message of Catholic social teaching is not to be found in one place. It is composed of a dozen major papal statements from 1891 to 1991, documents from the Second Vatican Council (1962-1965), the proclamation of the 1971 international meeting of bishops, and the papers from regional and national conferences of bishops, especially in Latin America (1968 and 1979), Ireland (1977), and the United States (1983, 1986, and 1988).[5]

The first official Catholic statement in the realm of formal "social teaching" is commonly regarded as Pope Leo XIII's 1891 encyclical letter *Rerum Novarum* ("On the Condition of Working People"). Customarily, papal pronouncements take their Latin titles from their opening words. In this case, the *"rerum novarum"* (literally "on new things") to which Pope Leo was referring were the problems of industrialization. Metaphorically, however, the most significant "new thing" which this encyclical has represented is that it took the Catholic Church irreversibly into an active role in the social issues of the world.

"In the final analysis, all social thought is how people should treat one another," one Catholic observer has noted.[6] The Church sees as a central feature of its mission to teach people how to live in order to reach salvation with God. It is thus something of an anomaly that a 2,000-year-old institution would have developed a formal body of social thought only in the past century.

It was not that the Church had never had anything to say about human life or matters of the world. On the contrary. From the Bible, of course, it drew the Ten Commandments, largely on what conduct to avoid. It also pilloried Cain's self-serving question, "Am I my brother's keeper?" (Genesis 4:9)

Moreover, the Church highlighted the eight beatitudes of the Sermon on the Mount: blessing the poor in spirit, the meek, those that mourn, they that hunger and thirst after justice, the merciful, the clean of heart, the peacemakers, and those that suffer persecution for the sake of justice. (Matthew 5:3-10) It celebrated the parable of the Good Samaritan on the meaning of neighborliness (Luke 10:29-37) and taught Christ's dictum that the greatest commandment is to love God and to "love thy neighbor as thyself." (Mark 12:28-31)

In addition to its Biblical models, the Catholic Church also offered as moral guidelines for human behavior the theological virtues of faith, hope, and charity; the cardinal virtues of prudence, justice, fortitude, and temperance; and the corporal and spiritual works of mercy (among them, feeding the hungry and clothing the naked).

As for its actions in the world, the Church took on the mission of spreading the Gospel, but it was preoccupied for centuries with combatting heresy and schism, promoting the values of monasticism, mobilizing the Crusades, countering the Reformation, and dealing with princes to protect its institutional interests. Popes occasionally made pronouncements on public issues. (In 1139, Pope Innocent II condemned the lethal crossbow as "hateful and unfit for Christians" but later modified his edict to permit its use against Muslims.)[7] The influential Augustine of Hippo and Thomas Aquinas developed the concept of "just" and "unjust" wars, but both left what some modern commentators consider a negative legacy on Catholic social thought.

For example, historian Thomas Bokenkotter finds in Aquinas (1225-1274) — despite the achievement of his *Summa Theologica* — "a social ethic that canonized the *status quo*. Social obligations were stressed at the expense of individual human rights. . . . A host of social evils — slavery, male domination, war, poverty, etc. — were all considered part of immutable natural law, which regulated human relationships in a world corrupted by original sin."[8]

Moreover, theologian Joseph Gremillion considers Augustine (354-430) the architect of the unnatural separation between things of the spirit and things of the world. "His sharp dichotomy between the City of God and the

City of Man concretized the mind-set of Western history for over thirteen hundred years," he writes.[9] That is, the Catholic Church usually confined its pronouncements to other-worldly matters rather than the temporal issues of human society. Irish theologian Donal Dorr notes that many past popes spoke in "escapist" terms, endorsing earthly suffering in the hope of heavenly reward.[10]

Even Pope Leo XIII, who would initiate a new direction for the Church in formal social teaching, took the position (at least in 1878, his first papal year) that political injustices could be challenged only by patience and prayer:

> And if at any time it happen that the power of the State is rashly and tyrannically wielded by princes, the teaching of the Catholic Church does not allow an insurrection on private authority against them, lest public order be only the more disturbed, and lest society take greater hurt therefrom. And when affairs come to such a pass that there is no other hope of safety, she teaches that relief may be hastened by the merits of Christian patience and by earnest prayers to God.[11]

Nowadays, the Catholic Church takes a sharply different approach. With Leo XIII's 1891 *Rerum Novarum*, in theologian Richard McBrien's view, it began "to articulate in a consciously *systematic* manner a theology of *social justice* and all that this implies."[12] It makes no apology about the appropriateness of its teachings on political, economic, and social questions. The current pope, John Paul II, emphasizes what Dorr calls an "integral humanism embracing all dimensions of life," which rejects "the old-fashioned dualist theology that would justify an 'escape' by Christians from social and political involvement."[13] John Paul himself has said that "the Church considers this concern for human beings, for their humanity, for the future of the human race on earth and therefore also for the direction of the totality of development and progress — to be inextricably linked to the Church's own mission and an essential element of it."[14]

The Underlying Principle

The principle on which all Catholic social teaching rests is the dignity of each individual person made in the image of God. The Church's social documents are replete with references to this fundamental point.

Pope John XXIII took individual dignity as the basis for his analysis of human rights, and the Second Vatican Council opened its principal document with a chapter on "The Dignity of the Human Person." Leo XIII based his discussion of workers' rights on the same principle, and even the aristocratic Pius XII, last of the pre-Vatican II pontiffs and one who wrote no social encyclicals, made personal dignity a regular theme of his radio addresses.

The American Catholic Bishops summed up this principle in their 1983 pastoral letter:

> . . . at the center of all Catholic social teaching are the transcendence of God and the dignity of the human person. The human person is the clearest reflection of God's presence in the world; all of the Church's work in pursuit of both justice and peace is designed to protect and promote the dignity of every person.[15]

It is this principle of human dignity which is the driving force behind the most visible, passionate, and controversial campaign with which Catholics are publicly identified today: the pro-life movement and its efforts against abortion. This is only one part, however, of a comprehensive "right-to-life" philosophy: that the quality of life in every respect should reflect human dignity. Thus Catholics who picket a clinic which performs abortions, peace marchers demonstrating against nuclear weapons, those who hand out leaflets in a farm workers' union boycott, organizers working for civil rights legislation, volunteers at a spouse abuse shelter — all are participating in the Catholic right-to-life program.

Furthermore, Catholics have an optimistic attitude about human nature. An illustration is the popular Christian hymn *Amazing Grace!* In the common version, the opening words are: "Amazing Grace! How sweet the sound that saved *a wretch like me!*" Catholics sing a different phrasing: "Amazing Grace! How sweet the sound that saved *and set me free!*"[16] Catholics believe that people are sinful and in need of redemption, but they are not taught to see themselves as "wretches." They consider themselves (and everyone else) the People of God.

Moreover, they are taught that human dignity requires what theologian McBrien calls "a coexistence of service."[17] As Christ enjoined as the standard for Final Judgment: ". . . as often as you did it for one of my least brothers, you did it for me . . . as often as you neglected to do it for one of these least ones, you neglected to do it to me." (Matthew 25:31-46)

In his letter "On Social Concerns" (1987), John Paul II underscored this point with a particularly forceful call for individual responsibility and action in every case of injustice: "At stake is the *dignity of the human person*, whose *defense* and *promotion* have been entrusted to us by the Creator, and to whom the men and women at every moment in history are strictly and responsibly *in debt*."[18]

The Essence of Catholic Social Teaching

Catholic social teaching stems from the Bible and tradition but it is most fully expressed in a diverse collection of church documents, especially the "social encyclicals" of various popes. Herein lies a major reason why so many Catholics are unfamiliar with the social doctrine of their church. Most papal letters are virtually unreadable. One commentator called them "jaw-breaker encyclicals," and the headline in a 1991 *National Catholic Reporter* column on the subject noted: "Have you ever met anyone who ever read an encyclical?"[19] The problem is more than a matter of linguistic translation. They are often poorly organized, excessively wordy, and intimidating in length (Pope John Paul II's *Centesimus Annus*, for example, running 114 pages). They defeat even the most earnest reader.

The encyclical *Pacem in Terris* ("Peace on Earth," 1963), however, is noteworthy for its readability. It is the place to start for a first-hand understanding of the gist of Catholic social teaching. Like its author Pope John XXIII, it is approachable, plain-spoken, and humanistic.

The title superficially suggests that the letter is another routine papal condemnation of war. Actually, it is a description of the kind of society — based on a full recognition of human rights — that Catholics and all men and women "of good will" are called upon to put into practice, and which will result in not merely the absence of war but the achievement of true "peace on earth."

Human dignity is the ultimate social basis:

> Any human society, if it is to be well ordered and productive, must lay as a foundation this principle, namely, that every human being is a person, that is, his nature is endowed with intelligence and free will. By virtue of this, he has rights and duties of his own, flowing directly

and simultaneously from his very nature, which are therefore universal, inviolable and inalienable.[20]

Proceeding from this point, the pope went on to note that every person has "the right to life, to bodily integrity, and to the means which are necessary and suitable for the proper development of life." Among others, he cited that all people have the right "to take an active part in public affairs," to freedom of movement between countries, "to choose freely the state of life which they prefer," to "a standard of living in keeping with human dignity," to a basic education, "to freedom in searching for truth," to artistic expression, to worship according to conscience, and to respect for their "good reputation."

Pope John made a particular point about the rights of women, calling the issue one of the "signs of the times": "Since women are becoming ever more conscious of their human dignity, they will not tolerate being treated as inanimate objects or mere instruments, but claim, both in domestic and in public life, the rights and duties that befit a human person."[21] That sentence would not have been out of place in Betty Friedan's *The Feminine Mystique,* which was also published in 1963 and is credited with helping to set in motion the women's movement.

Furthermore, he took note of the duties of citizenship, condemned racism, assailed the arms race, and called for a ban on nuclear weapons. And he appealed to the moral obligation of the wealthier countries to assist the underdeveloped world — a theme put forward in Barbara Ward's widely read *The Rich Nations and the Poor Nations* (1962).

In the course of his comments, Pope John made recurring references to two distinctly Catholic concepts: the "common good" and the "natural law." While not unique to Catholicism, these principles are significant in the Church's social teaching.

The common good is not merely "the greatest good of the greatest number." It is, in John XXIII's words, "the sum total of those conditions of social living," whereby people "are enabled more fully and more readily to achieve their own perfection" and "is chiefly guaranteed when personal rights and duties are maintained."[22]

Natural law is an ethical standard which "the Creator of the world has imprinted in man's heart" and "which his conscience reveals to him and enjoins him to obey."[23] In contrast to past Church use of this concept to defend the status quo, current Catholic social teaching takes a "dynamic" interpretation of natural law: institutions should be challenged and changed whenever they are inconsistent with human dignity.[24]

Pacem in Terris is an idealistic statement. It echoed the United Nations' Universal Declaration of Human Rights (1948) and it struck a familiar American chord in its recollection of the founding values of "life, liberty, and the pursuit of happiness" in the 1776 Declaration of Independence. Yet it was the first time the Catholic Church had laid out a detailed description of the kind of temporal society it sought. Subsequent popes and bishops would carry Catholic social teaching even further by emphasizing the restructuring of the social order.

The Development of Catholic Social Teaching

Formal Catholic social doctrine starts with *Rerum Novarum* ("On the Condition of Working People," 1891), the first papal encyclical to address a social issue. Pope Leo XIII's letter did not emerge suddenly from "on high." It bore the influence of a number of people who had been trying for decades to bring the "official" Church into the questions of the world.[25]

In *Rerum Novarum*, Leo condemned the use of workers as "mere instruments for making money" and spoke harshly of sweatshop free enterprise, whereby "a small number of very rich men have been able to lay upon the masses of the poor a yoke little better than slavery itself." The pope called for a "just wage," which he described as "enough to support the wage-earner in reasonable and frugal comfort" and to enable a worker "to put by a little property." He spoke for shorter hours and restrictions on child labor, and he endorsed trade unions. He also urged cooperation of the classes: "Each requires the other; capital cannot do without labor, nor labor without capital."

Furthermore, while he rejected socialism (a threat to "the inviolability of private property"), he issued a direct challenge to *laissez-faire* capitalism, the then-prevailing notion that the economy should function according to "natural laws" of the marketplace, with no government interference. He spurned the idea that a worker's mere acceptance of a wage relieved the employer of further obligations in justice, and he called for government intervention: "The richer population have many ways of protecting themselves; . . . those who are badly off . . . must chiefly rely upon the assistance of the State."[26]

By today's standards, some of what the pope said would not be characterized as progressive. He virtually "canonized" private property, in the view of some critics, in his effort to combat Marxism. He noted that women are "by nature fitted for home-work," and he said that workers' associations must consider "religion first" and pay "principal attention to piety and morality." He gave no encouragement to political action on the part of working people. What the pope was basically making, says

Donal Dorr, was a moral appeal to the powerful for "change from the top down rather than from the bottom up."[27]

Yet the encyclical was significant, especially on the Church's view of itself. One observer has commended it as the first time the labor movement "had received a stamp of approval from any of the great forces of order in the world."[28] Another considers it "particularly important, perhaps not so much because of its content as because it represented a decisive intervention by the pope in behalf of the poor."[29] An American bishop in 1891 caught its significance and remarked that now "the mission of the Church is not only to save souls, but also to save society."[30]

Rerum Novarum has been called the "Magna Carta" of Catholic social teaching.[31] Like that political document of 1215, it was the beginning of a significant pattern.

Such is the standing of *Rerum Novarum* that its anniversaries have become the occasions for popes to issue commemorations and social encyclicals of their own. Half of the popes' "social" encyclicals have been written in the decennial years of *Rerum Novarum*: 1931, 1961, 1971, 1981, 1991. Each recalled favorably the basic ideas of Leo XIII and the growing tradition of Catholic social teaching, while usually taking it further.

Pope Pius XI reestablished the practice of regular papal social encyclicals with *Quadragesimo Anno* ("In the Fortieth Year") in 1931. The Church had languished in this regard under the traditionalist Pius X and his successor Benedict XV. In America, the bishops had formed the National Catholic Welfare Council in 1919 and appointed the respected Monsignor John A. Ryan to head its Social Action Department to carry out the social justice teaching of the Church.[32] That same year, the U.S. hierarchy adopted the "Bishops' Program of Social Reconstruction." It was a progressive plan (drafted by Ryan) which foreshadowed many of the things enacted during Franklin Roosevelt's New Deal of the 1930s — and in the tradition of which the bishops' pastorals of the 1980s followed.

The Church's social message was still overshadowed by its long-time image as a defender of the status quo. In her autobiography, Dorothy Day (1897-1980) — who converted to Catholicism in 1926 and went on to co-found the Catholic Worker Movement and become a symbol of Church teaching on activism in behalf of human dignity — remarked that she had been oblivious to Catholic social justice principles:

> Not long afterward a priest wanted me to write a story of my conversion, telling how the social teaching of the Church had led me to embrace Catholicism. But I knew nothing of the social teaching of the Church at that time. I had never heard of the encyclicals. I felt that the Church was the Church of the poor, that St. Patrick's had been built from the pennies of servant girls, that it cared for the emigrant, it established hospitals, orphanages, day nurseries, houses of the Good Shepherd, homes for the aged, but at the same time I felt it did not set its face against a social order which made so much charity in the present sense of the word necessary. I felt that charity was a word to choke over. Who wanted charity? And it was not just human pride, but a strong sense of man's dignity and worth and what was due him in justice, that made me resent, rather than feel proud of, so mighty a sum of Catholic institutions.[33]

A turning point in Catholic social teaching — at which it began to identify itself more clearly with social change than social order and to rank its concern for justice more highly than its interest in stability — was John XXIII's 1961 *Mater et Magistra* ("Mother and Teacher").[34]

Pope John went further than his predecessors in stressing the social obligations of private property and endorsed government intervention along the welfare state model in the name of the common good. Pius XI had put forward the "principle of subsidiarity": essentially, the approach that government should never do for individuals what they can accomplish for themselves. John XXIII added the "principle of socialization": that the complexity of modern social problems has produced an interdependence which warrants a more activist government. This encyclical represented, says Dorr, "a decisive move away from the right" and "a major step in dissociating the Church from the forces in society that were most opposed to structural change."[35] Many traditionalist Catholics reacted negatively, as if to say: *"Mater si, Magistra no!"*[36]

The Second Vatican Council, which Pope John summoned to "throw open the windows" of the Church, went further still. The council provided wholesale "renewal," particularly on the values of participation and tolerance within and on the part of the Church itself. Its principal social document was "The Church in the Modern World" (*Gaudium et Spes*, literally "Joy and Hope," 1965). One theologian makes much of the significance of the phrase *"in* the World" rather than the Church " *and* the World."[37] Flowing from its role of integrating the spiritual and the temporal, the council emphasized that the "Church must be present to injustice."[38]

Prior to John XXIII and Vatican II, Catholic social teaching focused on industrial relations and had little to say about other issues. Since then its statements have taken, says one historian, a different direction and spirit:

> In these documents it is no longer a triumphant Church but a Church that wants to humbly serve the world; a Church no longer dubious about the value of human progress but one that applauds every human effort to build a better world; no longer a Church with all the answers, but a Church that seeks dialogue and admits that it can learn as well as teach . . . It is a Church that no longer speaks ambiguously about human liberty, but commits itself wholeheartedly to the struggle for greater human freedom and liberation of the oppressed.[39]

Pope Paul VI went a step beyond John XXIII by stressing the responsibility of government to assure justice and by endorsing the term "liberation," which emerged at the 1968 conference of Latin American Bishops in Medellin, Colombia. The pope called for "liberation from everything that oppresses people" and — while not sanctioning the "revolution" that the word had come to be associated with — legitimized it theologically by linking its temporal and spiritual aspects with an added reference to "liberation from sin and the Evil One."[40]

Finally, the most noteworthy development in recent years has been the endorsement of the concept of "a preferential option for the poor." It calls for the Church to examine social questions from the perspective of the poor and powerless. The phrase was coined in the final report of the Latin American Bishops' conference at Puebla, Mexico, in 1979; it turned up as a central feature of the U.S. Bishops' 1986 pastoral letter *Economic Justice for All*; and it was cited by Pope John Paul II in his encyclical "On Social Concerns" (1987).[41]

Pope John Paul has an image of stern doctrinal orthodoxy, but McBrien considers him "to the left of the U. S. bishops" on most social questions (except the concerns of women).[42] He has emphasized the "solidarity" of the oppressed, encouraged the poor to be the principal agents of their own liberation, and condoned the idea of a "struggle" for justice (a point downplayed by popes like Leo XIII). He has also noted that the Church does not advocate a "third way" between "liberal capitalism and Marxist collectivism" — rather, it stands for social justice in judging institutions "solely for the human being."[43]

What Is Justice?

Since the time of Thomas Acquinas, the Catholic Church has distinguished three types of justice: "commutative justice" on the contractual obligations between individuals; "distributive justice" between a government and its people in the fair allocation of benefits and burdens; and "legal justice" on the duties of citizens toward the state and the community.[44]

"Social justice" is a phrase which has appeared only in the past half-century of Catholic social teaching. Pius XI was the first to use it, but neither he nor any of his successors defined it specifically. The American Bishops referred to it as "what is right."[45] Pope John Paul spoke of "that law of justice which ordains that every person should receive his due."[46] It has been described as "a concept still evolving" and its meaning has been the subject of much discussion.[47] But the 1977 Conference of the Bishops of Ireland cut through the debate with this plainspoken comment:

> Justice is about my work, my business, my commercial dealings, my profession, my style of life. Justice is about paying a just and fair wage for a

job, and doing a just and honest job for the wage. Justice is about buying and selling. It is about employing men and women or making them redundant. Justice is about meeting my contracts, promising and delivering what I promise at the promised time. Justice is about fair prices and just profits. It is about honesty and truthfulness and straight dealing in work, in business, in public service, in political life.[48]

In its focus on human dignity, the Catholic understanding of social justice echoes Martin Luther King's comment on the difference between "just" and "unjust" laws: "Any law that uplifts human personality is just. Any law that degrades human personality is unjust."[49] A useful definition of social justice was put forward in a recent pamphlet on Catholic social teaching: "all persons by virtue of being human have a right to the basic necessities for a *dignified* human life, and society as a whole has a duty to assist them in attaining that right."[50]

What Authority? How Compulsory?

There is a relative weight attached to official documents of the Catholic Church. The opinion of a single bishop is not the same as a report from an ecumenical council; a statement from a group of auxiliary bishops is not the same as a pronouncement from the pope. The pope is the most important minister in the Church, but the pope alone does not speak for the Church. Since the Second Vatican Council, authority has been seen as collegial: the pope has primacy and exercises supreme authority, but the bishops share in it with a teaching authority of their own. The most authoritative Catholic statements are those from Church councils. Next weight are those from international synods of bishops, followed by papal encyclicals, and pastoral letters from conferences of bishops. Thereafter are less formal statements by the pope, and reports from committees of bishops.[51]

None of the Catholic body of social teaching has been presented as "infallible," but all of it bears the stamp of Church authority. Vatican II held that Catholics owe "religious allegiance of the will and intellect" to all papal statements.[52] The U.S. Bishops have said that "the moral judgments that we make in specific cases, while not binding in conscience, are to be given serious attention and consideration by Catholics as they determine whether their moral judgments are consistent with the Gospel."[53] For Catholics, "conscience is the final norm of moral action."[54] But as John XXIII urged in *Mater et Magistra*, the social teaching of the Church should receive "more and more attention" from the faithful.

Summary

These are the central points of Catholic social teaching:

1. The concern of the Catholic Church is for both the temporal and the spiritual welfare of people.

2. Human dignity is the underlying principle of its social teaching.

3. In the past century of formal social teaching, the Church has shifted from an emphasis on charity to a focus on justice, from a posture of support for the status quo to the encouragement of social change, from moral appeals to the powerful to animation of the powerless for structural reform.

4. Catholics are called upon to take personal action in all cases of social injustice — whenever the practices and structures of society are inconsistent with human dignity.

Endnotes

[1] Pope Paul VI, *World Day of Peace Message* (1972) in Gerald Darring (editor), *A Catechism of Catholic Social Teaching*, Kansas City, Mo.: Sheed and Ward, 1987, p. 97.

[2] Synod of Bishops, *Justice in the World*, #6 in Vincent P. Mainelli (editor), *Social Justice! The Catholic Position*, Washington, D.C.: Consortium Press. 1975, #1043.

[3] Michael J. Schultheis, Edward P. DeBerri, and Peter J. Henriot, *Our Best Kept Secret: The Rich Heritage of Catholic Social Teaching*, Washington, D.C.: Center of Concern, 1987, p. 7. David O'Brien also used the phrase in "Catholic Social Teaching: Remembrance and Commitment," *New Catholic World*, Vol. 229, No. 1373, September/October 1986, p. 228.

[4] "*New Catholic World* interviews businessman James Dunseith," *New Catholic World*, *op. cit.*, pp. 226-227. 5 Richard P. McBrien, *Catholicism: Study Edition*, Minneapolis: Winston, 1981, p. 938. Matthew Habiger, O.S.B., "The Antecedents and Central Claims of *Rerum Novarum*," *Social Justice Review*, Vol. 82, No. 5-6, May/June 1991, p. 77. In his 1991 centennial anniversary encyclical *Centesimus Annus*, Pope John Paul II credited *Rerum Novarum* as the start of Catholic social teaching. Apart from the papers of regional and national bishops' conferences, most authorities list these as the principal sources of Catholic social teaching, following Leo XIII's encyclical: Pope Pius XI, *Quadragesimo Anno* ("On Reconstructing the Social Order," 1931); Pope John XXIII, *Mater et Magistra* ("Christianity and Social Progress," 1961) and *Pacem in Terris* ("Peace on Earth," 1963); Second Vatican Council, *Gaudium et Spes* ("The Church in the Modern World," 1965); Pope Paul VI, *Populorum Progressio* ("On the Development of Peoples," 1967), *Octogesima Adveniens* ("A Call to Action," 1971), and *Evangelii Nuntiandi* ("Evangelization in the Modern World," 1975); Synod of Bishops, *Justice in the World* (1971); and Pope John Paul II, *Redemptor Hominis* ("Redeemer of Humankind," 1979), *Laborem Exercens* ("On Human Work," 1981), *Sollicitudo Rei Socialis* ("On Social Concerns," 1987), and *Centesimus Annus* ("The One Hundredth Year," 1991). Brief summaries of these documents are presented in *Shaping a New World: The Catholic Social Justice Tradition, 1891-1991*, Washington, D.C.: NETWORK, 1991, and Schultheis *et. al., op. cit.*

[6] John T. Joyce, "Reflections on Catholic Social Thought from a Labor Perspective," *New Catholic World*, *op. cit.*, p. 204.

[7] Bernard and Fawn Brodie, *From Crossbow to H-Bomb*, Bloomington: Indiana University, 1973, pp. 35-36.

[8] Thomas Bokenkotter, *Essential Catholicism: Dynamics of Faith and Belief*, Garden City, N.Y.: Doubleday, 1985, p. 358.

[9] Joseph Gremillion, (editor), *The Gospel of Peace and Justice: Catholic Social Teaching Since Pope John*, Maryknoll, N.Y.: Orbis, 1976, p. 4.

[10] Donal Dorr, *Option for the Poor: A Hundred Years of Vatican Social Teaching*, Maryknoll, N.Y.: Orbis, 1983, p. 135.

[11] Pope Leo XIII, *Quod Apostolici Muneris* (1878) in Etienne Gilson (editor), *The Church Speaks to the Modern World: The Social Teachings of Leo XIII*, Garden City, N.Y.: Doubleday, 1954, p. 194.

[12] McBrien, p. 938.

[13] Dorr, p. 218.

[14] Pope John Paul II, *Redemptor Hominis* (1979), #15 in Dorr, p. 218.

[15] National Conference of Catholic Bishops, *The Challenge of Peace: God's Promise and Our Response*, Washington, D.C.: United States Catholic Conference, 1983, #15, p. 6.

[16] Mark G. Rachelski and James E. Wilbur (editors), *We Celebrate*, Schiller Park, Ill.: J.S. Paluch, 1990, #116.

[17] McBrien, p. 144.

[18] Pope John Paul II, *Sollicitudo Rei Socialis* (1987), #47 in *The Pope Speaks*, Vol. 33, No. 2 (1988), p. 153.

[19] Gremillion, p. 68. Michael O. Garvey, "Have you ever met anyone who ever read an encyclical?" *National Catholic Reporter*, May 31, 1991, p. 13.

[20] Pope John XXIII, *Pacem in Terris* (1963), #9 in Ronald Staley, *Catholic Principles of Social Justice*, Los Angeles: Lawrence, 1964, p. 45.

[21] *Pacem in Terris*, #11-26, 41 in Gremillion, pp. 203-206, 209-210.

[22] Pope John XXIII, *Mater et Magistra* (1961), #65 in Gremillion, p. 157. *Pacem in Terris*, #60 in Staley, p. 62.

[23] *Pacem in Terris*, #5 in *ibid.*, p. 44.

[24] Gremillion, pp. 9-10.

[25] Fr. Matteo Liberatore, S.J. wrote the first draft of *Rerum Novarum* and Cardinal Thoma Zigliara, O.P. the second. Bishop Wilhelm von Ketteler of Mainz had influence on the pope, as did James Gibbons, the pro-labor U.S. cardinal who wrote Leo XIII a long letter on the Knights of Labor in 1887. Habiger, p. 78. Aaron I. Abell, *American Catholicism and Social Action*, Garden City, N.Y.: Doubleday, 1960, pp. 67-73. George Higgins, "The Catholic Church and Labor in the United States," *New Catholic World*, *op. cit.*, p. 199.

[26] Pope Leo XIII, *Rerum Novarum* (1891), #2, 12, 15, 29, 33-37 in Anne Freemantle (editor), *The Social Teaching of the Church*, New York: New American Library, 1963, pp. 22, 27-28, 30, 42, 44-50.

[27] *Ibid.*, #33, 42, pp. 45, 52. Dorr, p. 19. Oswald Von Nell-Breuning, S.J., "*Rerum Novarum* — A General Appraisal," *Social Justice Review*, *op. cit.*, p. 76. Nell-Breuning refutes the charge that private property was "canonized."

[28] Roger Aubert, quoted in Bokenkotter, p. 361.

[29] Dorr, p. 205.

[30] Bishop John Lancaster Spalding, quoted in Abell, p. 77.

[31] Schultheis *et. al.*, p. 11. Habiger, p. 77.

[32] Abell, pp. 199, 209-211. Ryan had written *A Living Wage* in 1906, regarded as "the *Uncle Tom's Cabin* of the minimum wage movement." He concluded that the average family could not live decently on less than $600 a year, and that at least 60% of heads of families earned less (pp. 88-89). James E. Hug, "Measuring the Shock Waves: The Economic Pastoral," *New Catholic World*, *op.cit.*, p. 215.

[33] Robert Ellsberg (editor), *By Little and By Little: The Selected Writings of Dorothy Day*, New York: Knopf, 1983, p. 39.

[34] Dorr, pp. 115, 263. Dorr credits Pius XI with the emphasis on justice over stability.

[35] *Ibid.*, p. 256. See McBrien, pp. 1043-1045 on "subsidiarity" and "socialization."

[36] Rupert J. Ederer, "On *Rerum Novarum* and Recidivism," *Social Justice Review, op. cit.*, p. 98. Dorr, p. 107. The translation is: "Mother yes, teacher no!"

[37] McBrien, p. 83.

[38] Schultheis *et. al.*, p. 50.

[39] Bokenkotter, p. 365.

[40] Quoted in Dorr, pp. 193-194. McBrien, p. 1046.

[41] Dorr, pp. 209-213, 224-225, 258-259. National Conference of Catholic Bishops, *Economic Justice for All: Pastoral Letter on Catholic Social Teaching and the U.S. Economy*, Washington, D.C.: United States Catholic Conference, 1986, #52, 85-91, pp. 28, 44-47. *Sollicitudo Rei Socialis*, #42 in *op. cit.*, p. 149. The influence of the Latin American Church should not be considered disproportionate. Of the world's 919 million Catholics, Brazil ranks first with 129.6 million and Mexico is next with 80.5 million, followed by Italy, the United States (54.9 million), and the Philippines. *The Florida Catholic*, July 19, 1991, p. 1; August 2, 1991, p. 20.

[42] Richard P. McBrien, "Papal, Bishops' ships 'passed in the night,'" *National Catholic Reporter*, October 2, 1987.

[43] *Sollicitudo Rei Socialis*, #41 in *op. cit.*, p. 149. Dorr, pp. 217, 259-260. Bokenkotter, p. 372. So broad have John Paul's comments on economic systems been that his latest encyclical *Centesimus Annus* (1991) drew praise from both the conservative theologian Michael Novak and the progressive Archbishop Rembert Weakland, O.S.B. *The Florida Catholic*, May 10, 1991, p. 12.

[44] McBrien, p. 985. William J. Drummond, S.J., *Social Justice*, Milwaukee: Bruce, 1955, pp. 15-16.

[45] National Conference of Catholic Bishops, *op. cit.*, #39, p. 22.

[46] *Centesimus Annus*, #10 in *National Catholic Reporter*, May 24, 1991, p. 19.

[47] Drummond, p. 19.

[48] Quoted in Oliver Mahoney, "Catholic Social Teaching — Ideal and Reality," *Studies*, Autumn 1987, p. 292.

[49] Martin Luther King Jr., "Letter from Birmingham City Jail" (1963) in Robert L. Brandfon (editor), *The American South in the Twentieth Century*, New York: Crowell, 1967, p. 173.

[50] Ted Thomas, *Catholic Social Teachings: Principles and Characteristics*, Columbus, Ohio: Commission on Peace and Justice, 1981, p. 2.

[51] McBrien, pp. 704, 834-836. Darring, p. vi.

[52] Second Vatican Council, *Lumen Gentium* (1964), quoted in McBrien, p. 841.

[53] National Conference of Catholic Bishops, *The Challenge of Peace*, #10, p. 5.

[54] McBrien, p. 1012.

The Challenge of Peace: God's Promise and Our Response (1983)

Excerpted by Jeanine Jacob

At the center of the Church's teaching on peace and at the center of all Catholic social teaching are the transcendence of God and the dignity of the human person. The human person is the clearest reflection of God's presence in the world; all of the Church's work in pursuit of both justice and peace is designed to protect and promote the dignity of every person. (#15)

The Catholic tradition has always understood the meaning of peace in positive terms. Peace is both a gift of God and a human work. It must be constructed on the basis of central human values: truth, justice, freedom, and love. The *Pastoral Constitution* [of the Second Vatican Council] states the traditional of peace:

Peace is not merely the absence of war. Nor can it be reduced solely to the maintenance of a balance of powers between enemies. Nor is it brought about by dictatorship. Instead, it is rightly and appropriately called "an enterprise of justice" (Is. 32:17). Peace results from that harmony built into human society by its divine founder and actualized by men as they thirst after ever greater justice. (#68)

The Christian has no choice but to defend peace, properly understood, against aggression. This is an inalienable obligation. It is the *how* of defending peace which offers moral options. (#73)

Pope Pius XII is especially strong in his conviction about the responsibility of the Christian to resist unjust aggression:

A people threatened with an unjust aggression, or already its victim, may not remain passively indifferent, if it would think and act as befits a Christian. All the more does the solidarity of the family of nations forbid others to behave as mere spectators, in any attitude of apathetic neutrality. (#76)

None of the above is to suggest, however, that armed force is the only defence against unjust aggression, regardless of the circumstances. (#77)

We believe work to develop non-violent means of fending off aggression and resolving conflict best reflects the call of Jesus both to love and to justice. (#78)

The moral theory of the "just-war" or "limited-war" doctrine begins with the presumption which binds all Christians: we should do no harm to our neighbors; how we treat our enemy is the key test of whether we love our neighbor . . . (#80)

The essential [just-war] position was stated by Vatican II: "As long as the danger of war persists and there is no international authority with the necessary competence and power, governments cannot be denied the right of lawful self-defense, once all peace efforts have failed." (#82)

Just-war teaching has evolved, however, as an effort to prevent war; only if war cannot be rationally avoided, does the teaching then seek to restrict and reduce its horrors. It does this by establishing a set of rigorous conditions which must be met if the decision to go to war is to be morally permissible. . . . It is presumed that all sane people prefer peace, never *want* to initiate war, and accept even the most justifiable war only as a sad necessity. Only the most powerful reasons may be permitted to override such objection. (#83)

Why and when recourse to war is permissible. (#85)

a)Just Cause: War is permissible only to confront "a real and certain danger," i.e., to protect innocent life, to preserve conditions necessary for decent human existence, and to secure basic human rights. (#86)

b)Competent Authority: . . . [W]ar must be declared by those with responsibility for public order, not by private groups or individuals. (#87)

c)Comparative Justice: . . . Every party to a conflict should acknowledge the limits of its "just cause" and the consequent requirement to use *only* limited means in pursuit of its objectives. Far from legitimizing a crusade mentality, comparative justice is designed to relativize absolute claims and to restrain the use of force even in a "justified" conflict. (#93)

d)Right Intention: . . . During the conflict, right intention means pursuit of peace and reconciliation, including avoiding unnecessarily destructive acts or imposing unreasonable conditions (e.g., unconditional surrender). (#95)

e)Last Effort: For resort to war to be justified, all peaceful alternatives must have been exhausted. (#96)

f)Probability of Success: . . . [I]ts purpose is to prevent irrational resort to force or hopeless resistance when the outcome of either will clearly be disproportionate or futile. (#98)

g)Proportionality: . . . [T]he damage to be inflicted and the costs incurred by war must be proportionate to the good expected by taking up arms. (#99)

Precisely because of the destructive nature of nuclear weapons, strategies have been developed which previous generations would have found unintelligible. Today military preparations are undertaken on a vast and sophisticated scale, but the declared purpose is not to use the weapons produced. Threats are made which would be suicidal to implement. (#136)

The political paradox of deterrence has also strained our moral conception. May a nation threaten what it may never do? May it possess what it may never use? (#137)

Under no circumstances may nuclear weapons or other instruments of mass slaughter be used for the purpose of destroying population centers or other predominantly civilian targets. (#147)

We do not perceive any situation in which the deliberate initiation of nuclear warfare, on however restricted a scale, can be morally justified. Non-nuclear attacks by another state must be resisted by other than nuclear means. Therefore a serious moral obligation exists to develop non-nuclear defense strategies as rapidly as possible. (#150)

No society can live in peace with itself, or with the world, without a full awareness of the worth and dignity of every human person, and of the sacredness of all human life (Jas. 4:1-2). When we accept violence in any form as commonplace, our sensitivities become dulled. When we accept violence, war itself can be taken for granted. (#285)

After the passage of nearly four decades and a concomitant growth in our understanding of the ever growing horror or nuclear war, we must shape the climate of opinion which will make it possible for our country to express profound sorrow over the atomic bombing in 1945. Without that sorrow, there is no possibility of finding a way to repudiate future use of nuclear weapons or of conventional weapons in such military actions as would not fulfill just-war criteria. (#302)

Bernard S. Parker

The Catholic Bishops on Nuclear Deterrence and the Just War Tradition

The American Catholic Bishops' pastoral letter on war and peace was published in 1983 after three years of drafts and discussions involving a wide array of professionals both Catholic and non-Catholic.[1] It is a new policy statement dealing with the complex moral issues of nuclear armaments but it is sensitive to the long philosophical and theological traditions of just war theory. Notre Dame's President Theodore Hesburgh called it "the finest document that the American Catholic hierarchy has ever produced."[2]

Entitled *The Challenge of Peace: God's Promise and Our Response,* the pastoral is divided into four parts: 1)the scriptural and historical foundations underlying the moral choices in considering the option of war; 2)the moral principles to be considered for a policy of nuclear deterrence; 3)policies related to disarmament and suggestions for shaping a peaceful world; and 4)a call for prayer and penance with suggested educational programs to promote peace in the world.

The pastoral was written because, in the bishops' words "the world is at a moment of crisis . . . nuclear war threatens the existence of our planet."(#2,3) They hope to generate conscious choices to face this challenge.

Overview

In Part One of the pastoral, the bishops discuss "both the religious vision of peace among people and nations and the problems associated with realizing this vision in a world of sovereign states."(#20)

The role that war and peace played in both the Old and New Testament is examined but, say the bishops, it is "clear that they do not provide us with detailed answers to the specifics of the questions which we face today."(#55) They present an analysis of the nature of peace and the criteria demanded for a just war.

Part II takes up the most critical issues raised by the pastoral: establishing moral guidelines to address not only the use of nuclear weapons but also a policy of nuclear deterrence. This section concludes with a discussion of the moral principles and policy choices related to: "1)the targeting doctrine and strategic plans for the use of the deterrent, particularly their impact on civilian casualties; and 2)the relationship of deterrence strategy and nuclear war-fighting capability to the likelihood that war will in fact be prevented."(# 177)

In the third part of the pastoral, the bishops offer proposals and policies for promoting peace. Arms control, civil defense, and nonviolent means of conflict resolution are discussed as specific steps to reduce the danger of war. The letter notes that "keeping the peace in the nuclear age . . . does not solve or dissolve the other major problems of the day."(#259) The interdependence of the world demands attention to the protection of human rights and the sharing of resources.

The final section of the pastoral offers some practical programs to respond to the challenge posed by the pastoral. The reader is called to prayer and penance so that the words of the prophet Isaiah might be fulfilled:

If you do away with the yoke, the clenched fist,
the wicked word, if you give your bread to the
hungry and relief to the oppressed, your light will
rise in the darkness, and your shadows become
like noon. (Isaiah 58:6-8, 10)

The Task

The bishops have accepted a considerable challenge to
"undertake a completely fresh reappraisal of war." This
injunction of Vatican II is quoted three times in the pastoral. (#23, 66, 122) However, an underlying philosophical dilemma arises from their attempt to examine a policy
of nuclear deterrence within the context of the just war
tradition.

The way in which the bishops craft their position has
stimulated the public discussion of this issue, and as
theologian Phillip Berryman writes:

The ultimate test of the bishop's document is not
whether they persuade us to see things as they do,
but whether they aid us to become more engaged
in dealing with the fundamental issues of our
time in the quest for a peaceful world where all
persons can attain dignity and fulfillment.[3]

A central feature of the pastoral is the bishops' argument that the just war tradition does provide guidance in
making moral choices about the complex issues of modern
warfare.

Just War Tradition

The just war tradition relied upon by the pastoral is "the
logic of Augustine and Aquinas to articulate a right of
self-defense." (# 82) There are two components to this
just war theory — the *jus ad bellum* (the war-decision

component) and the *jus in bello* (the war-conduct component).

There are seven elements in the "war-decision" component and all must be present to justify the action morally:

1. The cause must be just.
2. The proper authority must make the decision to go to war.
3. A question of justice as grave as the prospect of war must be at issue.
4. The right intention must be present.
5. War must be a last resort.
6. There must be a high likelihood of success.
7. The good achieved must be in proportion to the destruction caused. (# 80-100)

There are two elements which must be present for the morality of the "war-conduct" component:

1. Discrimination: Indiscriminate killing of noncombatants is never permitted.
2. Proportionality: Whatever military action is taken must be proportionate to the good achieved. (#101-110)

All of these principles must be present for a war to be justified according to traditional just war theory.

President George Bush was so sensitive to this issue that he went out of his way to try to make a case that the 1991 Persian Gulf conflict was morally justifiable because it met the tests of the just war tradition.[4]

Few people disagreed with President Bush's claim that the Gulf War was sanctioned by proper authority, since both the Congress and the United Nations had authorized force. It was also widely agreed that the probability of success was high.

To stop further aggression by Iraq and liberate the people of Kuwait appeared to be just causes. The pastoral also cites as a just cause "to preserve conditions necessary for decent human existence." (#86)

The criterion of having the right intention is fulfilled if the reasons for the conflict are really those cited as a just cause. Many people claimed cheap oil was not a "right intention" to initiate war, although few would deny that to stop outright aggression was morally proper. The bishops also cite "blatant aggression from without" as one of the values critical enough to justify force and thereby fulfill the comparative justice criterion. (#94)

The two criteria that remain — last resort and proportionally — are the ones where disagreement with President Bush was sharpest. Bishop Walter F. Sullivan of Richmond, Virginia, urged citizens to examine whether the good achieved was proportionate to the damage done. During the forty-three day war, Iraq and Kuwait experienced "the most intensive bombing in military history," with estimates of the number of dead from 100,000 to 150,000 Iraqi soldiers and perhaps 50,000 Iraqi civilians.[5] Further "collateral damage" and the destruction of the infrastructure of Iraq raise serious concerns as to whether the conditions of proportionality were satisfied.

Pope John Paul II also denounced the Persian Gulf War as a "darkness" that "cast a shadow over the whole human community."[6] In summary, Bush's appeal to the traditional principles that justified going to war generated much disagreement.

Critics claimed the economic sanctions imposed would have achieved the same effect if given sufficient time and that therefore the "last resort" criterion was not fulfilled. The debate on proportionality which was waged prior to the conflict centered on the risks of nuclear war and the possibility of a broader conflict. The magnitude of the actual destruction of life and property combined with the environmental disaster became a significant part of assessing proportionality. This principle is not only a key in determining whether there was justification to go to war but must be present in the actual conduct of war. Was the economic, environmental, and human destruction equal to the good attained?

The other principle operative for the conduct of war to be justified is "discrimination." Some estimate that only a small proportion of the bombs deployed were of the "smart" type and that destruction was not limited to military targets. Noncombatant civilians were killed and estimates were that thousands of children may have become casualties as a result of the contamination of water and disruption of food supplies. There was much concern that the principle of discrimination was not fulfilled in the Gulf War.

Nuclear Deterrence

When the principles outlined above are applied to a policy of nuclear deterrence, the potential problem areas are not difficult to spot. These are the criteria of proportionality and discrimination. When the bishops reached into their moral arsenal of a just war theory to attempt to justify a policy of nuclear deterrence, they ran into difficulty with the system. One commentator writes, "Nuclear weapons explode the theory of just war. They are the first of mankind's technological innovations that are simply not encompassable within the familiar moral world."[7]

A policy of nuclear deterrence must be based on the actual intention to use nuclear weapons. Obviously if there is no intention ever to use the weapons then there is no deterrent effect in simply possessing them. A policy of nuclear deterrence, therefore, implies that the weapons will be used given the right conditions.

Traditional teaching assigns as much moral weight to real intentions as to tangible acts. If then, the actual use of nuclear weapons cannot be justified because such use would violate the war conduct principles of discrimination and proportionality, and if deterrence entails the intention to use such weapons, then it would seem to follow that a policy of nuclear deterrence cannot be morally justified.

The bishops clearly understand what a policy of nuclear deterrence means. They write that deterrence is "the dissuasion of a potential adversary from initiating an attack or conflict, often by the threat of unacceptable retaliatory damage."(#163) Therefore the acceptance of the morality of a policy of nuclear deterrence is also the acceptance of the morality of the *use* of nuclear weapons. And yet the bishops state that they see "no moral justification for submitting the human community to this risk."(#161)

This moral dilemma arises because the bishops accept as a premise not only that a country has a right to self defense but also an obligation to preserve the common good. If a nuclear deterrence policy did not entail the intention to use the weapons then the aggressor would not be deterred and therefore the common good would be threatened. Thus an inalienable duty would be violated and so the bishops find themselves in a moral dilemma which the pastoral never successfully resolves one way or another.

The main problem is that it appears likely that any actual use of nuclear weapons would violate the war-conduct principles of proportionality and discrimination — the latter because almost inevitably noncombatants would be killed if not by the direct blast then by the long-term effects of radiation.

The bishops are quite clear on the point that any use of nuclear weapons "which violate the principle of discrimination merits unequivocal condemnation."(#193) In addition, "the 'indirect effects' of initiating nuclear war are sufficient to make it an unjustifiable moral risk in any form." (#194)

Given these statements it is understandable why the bishops arrive at the conclusion they do: ". . . there must be no misunderstanding of our profound skepticism about the moral acceptability of any use of nuclear weapons." (#193) If they had applied the criteria within the just war tradition more stringently, they probably would have turned this skepticism into moral certainty. Instead they end up with "a strictly conditioned moral acceptance of nuclear deterrence." (#186)

Michael Quinlan highlights the problems of this position:

> The essence of the letter's apparent position on nuclear weapons is "possession for deterrence legitimate now, use always wrong." The letter nowhere explores the difficulties — indeed, nowhere admits clearly that there are difficulties — in such a stance, unprecedented in Christian ethical tradition. There is arguable a fundamental incoherence in the idea of deliberately maintaining a capability which must never be used. There are, however, also more concrete difficulties. The letter's position implies that if deterrence fails and non-nuclear resistance is then overborne, it is the unqualified duty of the defender to accept defeat; it assumes that deterrence based on an admitted bluff will indefinitely remain de-

pendable; and it requires the individuals directly
involved in sustaining deterrence to devote their
working lives to a schizophrenic task.[8]

The Dilemma and Some Concluding Observations

The dilemma posed by the pastoral becomes apparent
when the American Bishops' position on the actual use of
nuclear weapons and their position on nuclear deterrence
as amorally defensible policy are placed side by side:[9]

1. A policy of nuclear deterrence is morally acceptable
    (#178, #186) and since deterrence would only be
    effective if there is an intention to use nuclear
    weapons, then the intention to use such weapons is
    morally acceptable (#163).

2. Since it is clear that the use of nuclear weapons is
    not morally acceptable, then it follows that the in-
    tention to use such weapons is not morally accept-
    able (#188, #173, #167).

One can see that the two positions are not consistent
with one another because the intention to use nuclear
weapons is both morally acceptable and morally unacceptable. Thus by appealing to the traditional criteria for a
just war (both the *jus ad bellum* and the *jus in bello*) the
bishops have raised a dilemma.

How then can one escape from what is an untenable
position? Perhaps the problem rests with the traditional
just war criteria. Since the nature of modern warfare is
radically different from the weaponry of the Middle Ages
— the period when the just war theory was developed —
then one must radically alter the criteria for warfare. After
all, the moral criteria used in medieval times for the use
of money — when receiving interest on money was considered usury and therefore immoral — would not be
applicable for the complex financial dealings of today.

One might, for example, adopt as a criterion the necessity of taking a global community view. Given a serious threat to world human rights, then perhaps the indirect death of large numbers of noncombatants might be acceptable. This position might be strengthened if a theory of a populace's obligation to oppose its government in such a case were made clear.

Some redefinition might help to bolster the moral arsenal that is needed in moral decision-making. But such an approach would modify the traditional just war philosophy that has served well for centuries.

Another way out of this moral dilemma is to reconsider the connection between intentions and acts, as well as distinguish various gradations of intentions. Perhaps the moral currency of the two are so significantly different that one could deny any morality to an actual nuclear attack but give a limited nod to a policy of nuclear deterrence. Is there not some difference in guilt between the person who "intended" to harm another but was restrained by a third party, compared to the same person who "intended" to harm that person while thinking about it in a purely abstract way? Somewhere between these two intentions is the intention to use nuclear weapons under certain conditions within a policy of nuclear deterrence.

Despite its difficulties, the American Catholic Bishops' pastoral letter has succeeded in helping the public grapple with some of the fundamental moral issues facing the world.

Endnotes

[1]National Conference of Catholic Bishops, *The Challenge of Peace: God's Promise and Our Response*, Washington, D.C.: United States Catholic Conference, 1983. Citations are by paragraph number.

[2]Theodore Hesburgh, C.S.C., "Foreword" in *Catholics and Nuclear War*, edited by Philip J. Murnion, New York: Crossroads, 1983, p. vii.

[3]Phillip Berryman, *Our Unfinished Business*, New York: Pantheon, 1989, p. xv.

[4]George Bush, "Remarks at the Annual Convention of the National Religious Broadcasters," January 28, 1991, *Weekly Compilation of Presidential Documents*, Vol. 27, No. 5 (February 4, 1991), pp. 87-89.

[5] Thomas Mullen, "Catholic Bishop, in Column, Calls Gulf War a 'Massacre,'" *St. Petersburg Times*, May 11, 1991, p. 2e. A U.S. Census Bureau demographer was threatened with dismissal for publishing what were deemed "politically embarrassing" statistical estimates of Iraqui deaths in the Gulf War: 158,001, total – 86,194 men, 39,612 women, and 32,195 children. *St. Petersburg Times,* April 12, 14, 1992.

[6]"Pope Denounces Gulf War," *St. Petersburg Times*, April 1, 1991, p. 6A.

[7]Michael Walzer, *Just and Unjust Wars*, New York: Basic Books, 1977, p. 282.

[8]Michael Quinlan, "The Ethics of Nuclear Deterrence: A Critical Comment on the Pastoral Letter of the U. S. Catholic Bishops," *Theological Studies*, 48 (1987), p. 13.

[9]The development here is based on the suggestion of James McGray's comment in "Note, Nuclear Deterrence: Is the War-and-Peace Pastoral Inconsistent?" *Theological Studies*, 46 (1985), p. 703.

Joseph A. Cernik

The Bishops as Political Activists: The Pastoral Letter on War and Peace

The American Catholic Bishops' 1983 pastoral letter *The Challenge of Peace: God's Promise and Our Response* created a stir in American politics. With this statement, the bishops came close to becoming political partisans. Where the dividing line is between addressing moral issues and jumping overtly into politics is difficult to define. Archbishop Joseph Bernardin (later elevated to cardinal), who chaired the drafting committee, acknowledged the sensitivity but defended the bishops' action: "Because the nuclear war issue is not simply a political, but also a profoundly moral and religious question, the church must be a participant in the process of protecting the world and its people from the specter of nuclear destruction."[1]

The Emerging Political Critics

In January of 1981, the National Conference of Catholic Bishops (NCCB) formed an Ad Hoc Committee on War and Peace. This committee was to draft a statement which would be discussed at the annual bishops' meeting in November 1982. The first session of the committee was held in July 1981. The first draft was completed in May 1982, the second in October, and the final version was published in May 1983.

The central issue debated through the three drafts was over how strongly the bishops should express their opposition to the nuclear arms race.[2] A major feature concerned the use of the words "halt" versus "curb" in regard to the production of weapons. Should they call for a "halt" on such construction or merely a "curb," the bishops argued? The first draft used the word "halt," the second "curb," and the final version reinstated the term "halt."

This was more than just semantics. The use of one word or the other makes little sense unless understood as related to the type of message the bishops were sending regarding their role in politics. "Halt" would indicate a more aggressive public visibility and, therefore, political activism by the bishops, while "curb" would suggest a willingness to remain somewhat detached from the public debate on the nuclear arms race.

During the course of the writing of the three drafts of the pastoral, a number of bishops became vocal in their opposition to the military programs of President Ronald Reagan. *Newsweek* noted the emergence of the bishops as political activists: "Once the ruddy-cheeked epitome of patriotic 'fighting padres,' the American bishops have recently emerged as sharp critics of the arms race in general – and the Reagan Administration's politics in particular."[3] Bishop LeRoy Matthiesen of Amarillo, Texas told workers at a neutron bomb assembly plant that based on moral grounds they should consider other jobs. Archbishop Raymond Hunthausen stated he was withholding half of his 1981 federal income tax because of his opposition to the nuclear arms race.

After the release of the final version of the letter, 14 bishops issued a statement expressing their opposition to a specific Reagan administration nuclear weapons program: the MX intercontinental ballistic missile. They were reacting to congressional approval of funds for production of the first 21 of these missiles. Archbishops Bernardin and John O'Connor testified before a congressional committee in opposition to the MX. Both based their position on principles in the pastoral letter. In essence, the pastoral was seen as the foundation for political action.[4]

The pastoral letter as a political statement — not just a set of moral guidelines — can be examined in three ways. First, the letter itself was a call for political action. Second, the subsequent public discussion indicated both support and criticism of the letter, not just on its content but particularly related to the role the bishops were taking. And, third, the writing and revising of the letter cannot be divorced from the broader public debate then going on within American politics about the nuclear freeze issue.

A Pastoral Call for Political Action

The principal impetus behind the bishops' discussing war and peace was the election of Ronald Reagan as president.[5] Issues of war and peace had already drawn the attention of the bishops some years before, as evident by the 1976 release of the pastoral letter *To Live in Christ Jesus*, which criticized the nuclear weapons policy of attacking population centers. But "Reagan's election," said a noted national security journalist, "was the single greatest factor influencing the bishops."[6]

"We are called to be the peacemakers, not by some movement of the moment but by our Lord Jesus," the bishops wrote in the opening of *The Challenge of Peace* (1983).[7] Repeatedly, they used terms like "moment of crisis," "the signs of the times," and "moment of supreme crisis." (#2, 13, 4) This terminology suggests that something had changed from the time the bishops began their debate until the release of their final version. Their sense of urgency about the danger of a global nuclear war had intensified. While the bishops saw the arms race as a long-term feature of Soviet-American relations, the letter observed:

> What previously had been defined as a safe and stable system of [nuclear] deterrence is today viewed with political and moral skepticism. The nuclear age has been the theater of our existence for almost four decades; today it is being evaluated with a new perspective. (#125)

What had changed were two perceptions: 1)that achieving nuclear superiority over the Soviets was a goal of the Reagan administration; and 2)that the administration was willing to consider actually conducting a nuclear war. These perceptions prompted the bishops to reach for a broader audience.

Public opinion, the bishops explained in their letter, "indicate[s] the limits beyond which a government should not proceed." (#140) Their goal was to mobilize that opinion in order to challenge and reverse the perceived policies of the Reagan administration. Although reference is not made directly to President Reagan, it is apparent.

A centerpiece of their approach was an examination of the policy of nuclear deterrence. The bishops considered it a transitional policy, which meant that it was acceptable in the short run but was unacceptable as a permanent feature of international relations.

Such a policy rests on the premise that nuclear weapons might actually be used, since it is the threat to use them in a retaliatory strike that served to stabilize the military relationship between the United States and the Soviet Union. The notion that nuclear deterrence was acceptable as a transitional policy was supported by "just war" arguments raised in the letter. The theory of "just" and "unjust" wars is based on conditions that determine when it is acceptable for a nation to go to war and stipulations that restrain the conduct of war. In order to move away from nuclear deterrence as a permanent feature of international affairs, nations need to pursue arms control. It is through arms control that deterrence was seen "not as an end in itself but as a step on the way toward a progressive disarmament" and therefore it "may still be judged morally acceptable."[8]

Arms control involves a number of issues, and the bishops addressed them. Their pastoral supported not only a nuclear freeze but also proposals aimed at deep cuts in the nuclear arsenals of both the United States and the Soviet Union. In addition, the letter called for a comprehensive test ban treaty, as well as more controls on nuclear proliferation and limits on conventional arms.

Furthermore, the letter emphasized "defense by armed force if necessary as a last resort." (#75) Therefore, negotiations between belligerents should be comprehensive and exhaustive in order to find alternatives to war. The bishops recognized that there is a difference between a "peace of sorts" and "genuine peace," and that since the former is a reflection of international affairs, a nation might be caught in the dilemma of choosing between "justice" and "peace" — a situation which makes war an ever-present feature of world affairs. (#60, 61, 174, 175)

Finally, the pastoral recognized that "global interdependencies" existed, which meant that more weight should be given to the importance of the United Nations as an organization that can play a crucial role in an interdependent world. (#268)

It is the combination of viewing nuclear deterrence as a transitional policy and admitting the dilemmas that confront nations and individuals in choosing between peace and justice that forced the bishops toward becoming political participants.

The assumption that this document would be completed and left for others to interpret and act (or not act) upon, ignored the reasons that stirred the bishops to write it in the first place. The letter put the bishops in a sensitive position about their own role in public affairs. The debate over the three drafts of the letter was a prelude to the situation that the bishops found themselves in after the final version was released.

Politics is an activity filled with compromise, contradiction, choice, and uncertainty. Morality may be able to "stand above" politics and provide some ideal guidelines to evaluate human activity. But it cannot ignore the dilemmas that confront both individuals and governments if it is going to be of any practical assistance. This "caught-in-the-middle" situation between politics and morality could be understood by the confusion that came with the various reactions to the release of the letter.

Ambiguity is a noteworthy and deliberate feature of the pastoral, as NCCB President John Roach acknowledged: "I have come to the conclusion that ambiguity has a legitimate, treasured part of the whole moral tradition of the church. We develop some moral positions because we tolerate some ambiguity as we go along. That's the stage at which we are now."[9] Archbishop Bernardin endorsed this view, noting that "certain ambiguities" were deliberately left in the letter.[10]

Understandably then, public reaction to and interpretation of the pastoral was mixed. Moreover, the debate carried with it the underlying issue of the role the bishops would play in both attempting to influence American foreign policy as well as what role they might play in the upcoming 1984 presidential election.

Public Reaction to the Pastoral

Shortly after the completion of the second draft of the pastoral, two dozen Catholic members of Congress sent a letter to Archbishop Bernardin stating that they were opposed to any document that might speak of "disarm[ing] us in the name of peace."[11] Obviously, these members of Congress were concerned that the bishops' views would have an impact on public affairs. In fact, after the release of the final version of the letter, a *New York Times* editorial observed that the bishops came "perilously close to an undesirable involvement of the church in political action."[12]

Commentators on the letter tended to divide along lines of the bishops' position on arms control. For example, Herman Kahn, a noted strategic analyst and a critic of the bishops, said that the pastoral "reflects a sincere concern but an unenlightened simplicity."[13] George Kennan, a well-known authority on Soviet-American relations and a supporter of the bishops' position, called the letter "the most profound and searching inquiry yet conducted by any responsible collective body into the relations of nuclear weaponry, and indeed of modern war in general."[14]

Some supporters of the letter felt that the bishops had not gone far enough in criticizing nuclear war, a view expressed by Harold Agnew, former director of Los Alamos Scientific Laboratory.[15] Several critics, however, believed that the bishops had gone too far. Sidney Hook, for example, a senior research fellow at the Hoover Institution said that "the bishops' position is uninformed, unrealistic and morally irresponsible."[16]

The public debate over the letter cannot be separated from the broader debate that was going on regarding arms control and defense policy. In their pastoral letter, the bishops tried to disassociate themselves from specifically supporting the nuclear freeze movement. However, few saw the letter as a detached statement. In fact, both the development of the pastoral letter and the rise of the nuclear freeze movement were interrelated. Both grew as a result of opposition to Reagan administration defense policies.

The Nuclear Freeze Movement
and the Pastoral

The movement for a freeze on the production of nuclear weapons arose after the Strategic Arms Limitation Treaty was tabled by Congress in 1979. At that time, Senators George McGovern and Mark Hatfield pushed for congressional support on an amendment that would halt the development of nuclear weapons. This initial freeze effort drew little support.[17] The perception, however, that the Reagan administration had "a cavalier attitude toward the dangers of nuclear war and nuclear weapons" prompted the growth of a grass-roots movement in support of a nuclear freeze.[18]

The nuclear freeze movement began to gain strength by late 1981, during the same period that the first draft of the pastoral was being developed. On March 10, 1982, Senator Edward Kennedy and Representative Jonathan Bingham announced that they would introduce nuclear freeze resolutions in both houses of Congress. The years 1982 and 1983 were filled with both congressional and public debate as well as presidential reaction to this issue.

In the end, however, the movement faltered because Ronald Reagan was re-elected as president. Walter Mondale, the Democratic Party's challenger in the 1984 election, was somewhat inaccurately depicted as the champion of the nuclear freeze movement. Mondale favored the freeze, but at the same time supported the building of nuclear weapons. One of his major distinctions from President Reagan was that he advocated only a moderate increase in defense spending.

The bishops and their pastoral played a role in these developments, principally because of their potential ability to influence Catholic voters — a point not lost on either political party. Since the 1960s, the Catholic vote had begun to shift from the Democratic Party. In the 1980 election, 42 percent of the Catholic voters supported Jimmy Carter, the Democrat then in the White House, while 46 percent voted for Ronald Reagan. During the course of the debate within the Church hierarchy on the drafts of the letter, the White House tried to bring its influence to bear. After the release of the first draft, the administration attempted to get some of the language softened. William Clark, the president's national security adviser, wrote to Archbishop Bernardin that the bishops had ignored "previous administration comments that were forwarded to you" on "mistaken depictions of U.S. nuclear strategy."[19]

Partisan politics, however, was not the goal of the bishops. While reflecting criticism of Reagan administration's defense policies, the pastoral was not intended to provide a program to win Catholic voters back to the Democratic Party. As one journalist said: "The bishops . . . are hard to characterize politically."[20]

The Church hierarchy had been critical of President Reagan's defense policies, expressing a view which might have been translated into support for the Democrats. But the bishops were also strongly critical of abortion, taking a position that was closer to Reagan and the Republicans. For example, the pastoral linked nuclear weapons and abortion, in line with the traditional Catholic comprehensive "right-to-life" attitude:

> We must ask how long a nation willing to extend a constitutional guarantee to the "right" to kill defenseless human beings by abortion is likely to refrain from adopting strategic warfare policies deliberately designed to kill millions of defenseless human beings . . . (#288)

While it was Reagan administration defense policies that sparked the bishops to become more vocal regarding issues of war and peace, they tried to avoid taking a partisan position in discussing public affairs.

Conclusion

Throughout the debate within the Church hierarchy over the letter and during the period leading up to the 1984 presidential election, an uneasiness developed among the bishops regarding their role. This uneasiness could be seen in how different members interpreted the importance of the pastoral.

Bishop Maurice Dingham expressed the opinion that the pastoral reflected a situation wherein "we're now moving on the continuum from the just war theory over to pacifism and I think that reflects the general direction of the bishops. . . . [This] document reflects this movement."[21] Bishop Dingham's position implied that the bishops had reached a consensus regarding their public role and had chosen political activism. On the other hand, Cardinal John Krol labeled the pastoral as a "teaching document," implying that the members of the hierarchy were uncomfortable with the political role toward which they were moving.[22]

This question came to a head in August 1984 over the issue of abortion, when Governor Mario Cuomo of New York defended himself against charges made by Archbishop John O'Connor. The governor had made a statement that while he was personally opposed to abortion, he did not want to impose his personal views on individual members of the public. The archbishop responded that he could not see "how a Catholic in good conscience can vote for a candidate who explicitly supports abortion."[23]

Concerned that a line had been crossed, the National Conference of Catholic Bishops published a letter in which it urged Catholics to influence public issues but cautioned Catholic clergy to remain detached from partisan politics. NCCB President John Malone stated:

> The major problem the church has is internal. How do we teach? As much as I think we're responsible for advocating public policy issues, our primary responsibility is to teach our people. We're asking politicians to do what we haven't done effectively ourselves.[24]

By the end of 1984, Church leaders were still struggling over their role in public affairs, a situation which continues. The pastoral letter on war and peace, while a document that needs to be assessed in its own right, cannot be fully appreciated without reference to the broader political arena in which the letter was written and gained attention.

In his well-known work *Democracy in America*, Alexis de Tocqueville, a Frenchman who visited America in the 1830s, put his finger on the sensitivity of Catholic clerics in American politics:

The greatest part of British America was peopled by men who, after shaken off the authority of the Pope, acknowledged no other religious supremacy: they brought with them into the New World a form of Christianity which I cannot better describe than by styling it a democratic and republican religion. This contributed powerfully to the establishment of a republic and a democracy in public affairs; and from the beginning, politics and religion contracted an alliance which has never been dissolved. . . . It has not infrequently occurred that the Catholic priest has left the service of the altar to mix with the governing powers of society and to take his place among the civil ranks.[25]

If the bishops intend to continue issuing pastoral letters on public issues, it is difficult to see how they can avoid expressing their opinions and doing so in ways that will keep them detached from political activism.

Endnotes

[1] Marjorie Hyer, "Bishops Appear Divided on Proposed A-War Letter," *Washington Post*, November 16, 1982.

[2] Other issues were also addressed. The final version included a longer discussion on "just war" theory and stronger criticism of the Soviet Union for its role in helping to perpetuate the arms race. Furthermore, it used strong language critical of a "first use" policy. Weapons systems discussed in the text of the drafts (the MX and Pershing II missiles) were moved to the footnotes.

[3] "Churchmen Vs. the Bomb," *Newsweek*, January 11, 1982, p. 70.

[4] Richard Halloran, "Bishops Challenge MX in Testimony," *New York Times*, June 27, 1984.

[5] Jim Castelli, *The Bishops and the Bomb: Waging Peace in the Nuclear Age*, Garden City, N.Y.: Image Books, 1983.

[6] *Ibid.*, p. 15.

[7] *Ibid.*, "Summary," p. 194. The pastoral letter is reprinted in the Castelli book. Subsequent references are to paragraph numbers in the letter.

[8] *Ibid.*, "Summary," p. 190.

[9] "Those Disputatious Bishops," *New York Times*, November 24, 1982.

[10] Marjorie Hyer, "Poll Finds Most Bishops Agree With A-War Letter," *Washington Post*, November 17, 1982.

[11] "24 Catholics in the House Oppose Bishops on A-Arms,"*New York Times*, December 23, 1982.

[12] "The Bishops and the Bomb," *New York Times*, May 6, 1983.

[13] Herman Kahn, "Bishops and the Bomb," *New York Times*, December 8, 1982.

[14] George Kennan, "The Bishops' Letter," *New York Times*, May 6, 1983.

[15] "A Symposium: The Bishops and the Arms Race," *New York Times*, December 26, 1982.

[16] *Ibid.*

[17] Edward Feighan, "The Freeze in Congress," in Paul Cole and William Taylor, eds., *The Nuclear Freeze Debate: Arms Control Issues for the 1980s*, Boulder, Colorado: Westview Press, 1983.

[18] David Myer, *A Winter of Discontent: The Nuclear Freeze and American Politics*, New York: Praeger, 1990, p. 71.

[19] Marjorie Hyer, "U.S. Bishops Firm in the Pastoral Letter," *Washington Post*, November 18, 1982, and, Richard Halloran, "U.S. Tells Bishops Morally Is Guide On Nuclear Policy," *New York Times*, November 17, 1982. Halloran's article contains the full text of Clark's letter.

[20] Marjorie Hyer, "Bishops' A-War Paper Puts U.S. Catholics Into a New Court," *Washington Post*, November 2, 1982.

[21] "Is the Pastoral Letter on Nuclear Weapons Only a Beginning?" *New York Times*, May 8, 1983.

[22] Bill Prochnau, "Catholics Quandary Unresolved," *Washington* Post, May 8, 1983.

[23] Kenneth Briggs, "Leader of Catholic Bishops Drafts Statement Opposing Bipartisanship," *New York Times*, August 9, 1984.

[24] Kenneth Briggs, "Politics and Morality: Dissent in Catholic Church," *New York Times*, August 11, 1984.

[25] Alexis de Tocqueville, *Democracy in America*, Vol. 1, Phillips Bradley, ed., New York: Knopf, 1945, pp. 311-312.

Economic Justice For All: Pastoral Letter on Catholic Social Teaching and the U.S. Economy (1986)

Excerpted by Jeanine Jacob

Economic decisions have human consequences and moral content; they help or hurt people, strengthen or weaken family life, advance or diminish the quality of justice in our land. (Introduction #1)

The basis for all the Church believes about the moral dimensions of economic life is its vision of the transcendent worth — the sacredness — of human beings. *The dignity of the human person, realized in community with others, is the criterion against which all aspects of economic life must be measured.* [Pope John XXIII, *Mater et Magistra*, 219-220] All human beings, therefore, are ends to be served by the institutions that make up the economy, not means to be exploited for more narrowly defined goals. Human personhood must be respected with a reverence that is religious. . . . Similarly, all economic institutions must support the bonds of community and solidarity that are essential to the dignity of persons. Wherever our economic arrangements fail to conform to the demands of human dignity lived in community, they must be questioned and transformed. (#28)

Beginning in the first century and throughout history, Christian communities have developed varied structures to support and sustain the weak and powerless in societies that were often brutally unconcerned about human suffering. (#51)

Such perspectives provide a basis today for what is called the "preferential option for the poor." Though in the Gospels and in the New Testament as a whole the offer of salvation is extended to all peoples, Jesus takes the side of those most in need, physically and spiritually. (#52)

The virtues of citizenship are an expression of Christian love more crucial in today's interdependent world than ever before. These virtues grow out of a lively sense of one's dependence on the commonweal and obligations to it. This civic commitment must also guide the economic institutions of society. (#66)

Commutative justice calls for fundamental fairness in all agreements and exchanges between individuals and private social groups. It demands respect for the equal human dignity of all persons in economic transactions, contracts, or promises. (#69)

Distributive justice requires that the allocation of income, wealth and power in society be evaluated in light of its effects on persons whose basic material needs are unmet. . . . If persons are to be recognized as members of the human community, then the community has an obligation to help fulfill these basic needs unless an absolute scarcity of resources makes this strictly impossible. No such scarcity exists in the United States today. (#70)

Social justice implies that persons have an obligation to be active and productive participants in the life of society and that society has a duty to enable them to participate in this way. This form of justice can also be called "contributive," for it stresses the duty of all who are able to help create the goods, services and other nonmaterial or spiritual values necessary for the welfare of the whole community. (#71)

Economic conditions that leave large numbers of able people unemployed, underemployed, or employed in dehumanizing conditions fail to meet the converging demands of these three forms of basic justice. Work with adequate pay for all who seek it is the primary means for achieving basic justice in our society. (#73)

Catholic social teaching does not maintain that a flat, arithmetical equality of income and wealth is a demand of justice, but it does challenge economic arrangements that leave large numbers of people impoverished. Further, it sees extreme inequality as a threat to the solidarity of the human community, for great disparities lead to deep social divisions and conflict. (#74)

The full range of human rights has been systematically outlined by John XXIII in his encyclical *Peace on Earth.* . . . These rights include the civil and political rights to freedom of speech, worship, and assembly. A number of human rights also concern human welfare and are of a specifically economic nature. First among these are the rights to life, food, clothing, shelter, rest, medical care, and basic education. These are indispensable to the protection of human dignity. In order to ensure these necessities, all persons have a right to earn a living, which for most people in our economy is through remunerative employment. All persons also have a right to security in the event of sickness, unemployment, and old age. Participation in the life of the community calls for the protection of this same right to employment, as well as the right to healthful working conditions, to wages, and other benefits sufficient to provide individuals and their families with a standard of living in keeping with human dignity, and to the possibility of property ownership. . . . Any denial of these rights harms persons and wounds the human community. (#80)

Resources created by human industry are . . . held in trust. Owners and managers have not created this capital on their own. They have benefited from the work of many others and from the local communities that support their endeavors. They are accountable to these workers and communities when making decisions. (#113)

"Private property does not constitute for anyone an absolute or unconditioned right. No one is justified in keeping for his exclusive use what he does not need, when others lack necessities." [Pope Paul VI, *On the Development of Peoples*, 23] (#115)

[I]t is the responsibility of all citizens, acting through their government, to assist and empower the poor, the disadvantaged, the handicapped, and the unemployed. Government should assume a positive role in generating employment and establishing fair labor practices . . . The way society responds to the needs of the poor through its public policies is the litmus test of justice or injustice. (#123)

[D]oes our economic system place more emphasis on maximizing profits than on meeting human needs and fostering human dignity? Does our economy distribute its benefits equitably or does it concentrate power and resources in the hands of a few? Does it promote excessive materialism and individualism? Does it adequately protect the environment and the nation's natural resources? Does it direct too many scarce resources to military purposes? These and many other basic questions about the economy need to be scrutinized in the light of the ethical norms we have outlined. (#132)

S. Mary David Hydro, O.S.B.

An Introduction to the
Economic Pastoral

One of the Catholic Church's contributions to the economic debate of our time is *Economic Justice for All: Pastoral Letter on Catholic Social Teaching and the U.S. Economy.*[1] Published by the U.S. Bishops in 1986, it was the result of six years of consultation with economists, policy makers, and theologians.

The bishops' purpose in writing this pastoral was to add to the public debate over the direction of the U.S. economy and to help Catholics form a conscience about economic matters. The bishops make their central point clearly. The U.S. economy must not be measured by production only, but by its effects on people. What does the economy do to and for people? How do they participate in it? These questions are the litmus test of a moral economic life.

In the pastoral the bishops present a moral vision needed to address the "urgent problems" the U.S. economy must face; they challenge individuals and groups to take responsibility. The bulk of the letter deals with selected issues of concern and the bishops' suggested response to them. The pastoral gives a wealth of information about the economic conditions of American people and others linked to the U.S. economy, while it repeats principles and themes of earlier Catholic social teaching. The letter is firmly rooted in Scripture, the documents of Vatican II, and subsequent Catholic social teaching.

A Call to Conversion

In Chapter 1 the bishops define economics and its effects by quoting from the Vatican II document *The Pastoral Constitution on the Church in the Modern World* (#33): "The economy is a human reality: men and women working together to develop and care for the whole of God's creation . . . to serve the material and spiritual well-being of people. It influences what people hope for themselves and their loved ones. It affects the way they act together in society and their very faith in God."

Economic life is a chief place where one lives out faith. One's attitude and use of material goods will either help or hinder the reign of God. Economic choices raise fundamental questions of value and human purpose.

The U.S. economy is usually evaluated by its overall average performance in terms of production and consumption. Society generally sees economic activity as separate from moral considerations.

Concerned by the persistent failures of the economy, the bishops lay out an alternative analysis of the economic situation and call for change. The economy should be evaluated by the principle of inclusion that asks this: "What does the economy do to and for people and how does it serve the community?" The bishops challenge the separation of moral criteria and economic activity and state clearly that economic choices are moral choices. They insist on the centrality of work. They say government has a positive role to play.

Economic Justice for All is a call to conversion from an individualistic, materialistic economy where there is an imbalance of power as well as goods, to an economy based on the common good of society where the person is valued over things and every person can participate in the life of the community.

Wanted: A New Vision

"There is still unfinished business in the American experiment in freedom and justice for all." (#9) Writing as Americans, the bishops explicitly appeal to the creativity and imagination of the people of the United States when they call for "a new american experiment." If the essence of the American political genius was to bring about much more political participation than before, now is the time, the bishops explain, to extend those basic American policies to that of the economy. They ask for a national commitment to economic rights equal to that of civil rights.[2]

The bishops realize that the Bible cannot give solutions to today's complex economic questions, but they believe that it can shape a new vision. The biblical motifs of creation, covenant, and community are the basis of their views.

Each person is created by God with a human dignity and through work continues the Creator's work. God's covenant calls for each to participate responsibly in building a just community. Covenant with God is reflected in the responsibility, mercy, and truthfulness shown each other; that is, the justice of a nation is measured by its treatment of the powerless. Material things are good and are to be used for the good of all.

Basic Principles

Principles basic to a moral vision are outlined in the introduction to the pastoral.

1. "Every economic decision and institution must be judged in light of whether it protects or undermines the dignity of the human person."
2. "Human dignity can be realized and protected only in community."

3. "All people have a right to participate in the economic life of society."

4. "All members of society have a special obligation to the poor and vulnerable."

5. "Human rights are the minimum conditions for life in community."

6. "Society as a whole, acting through public and private institutions, has the responsibility to enhance human dignity and protect human rights." (Intro #13- 18)

These principles, reflecting over 100 years of social justice teaching, embody recurring and distinctively Catholic beliefs about the nature of persons and how they should live and work together in society.

Recurring Themes

Concepts found repeatedly in *Economic Justice for All* play key roles: human dignity, the common good, the role of government, the preferential option for the poor, the significance of work, and participation.[3]

Human dignity has been the foundation of all Catholic social teaching. As Vatican II noted, "the beginning subject and goal of all institutions is and must be the human person."

The common good is the second theme. Although this teaching emphasizes the individual, it sees the human person as a social being whose human rights are held in community. The common good is a set of social conditions that facilitate human development. It is a call for all to work responsibly for the general welfare of the entire human family.

Government exists to promote the common good and to enable people to live together in such a way as to develop their full personhood. As Pope John XXIII wrote in

Pacem in Terris: "Unless civil authorities take suitable action with regard to economic, political and cultural matters, inequities between citizens tend to become more widespread."

The concept of a preferential option for the poor is based on distributive justice. Pope Paul VI noted in *Populorum Progressio* that "when conflicts arise between those in need and those who are well-off, Catholic social teaching gives special priority to the needs of the poor. Such a preference aims precisely at liberating not just the poor, but all of humanity."[4]

"Work is probably the essential key in the whole social question," said Pope John Paul II in *On Human Work*. This encyclical gives a new direction to social justice as it states that the essence of human dignity is to be found in each person's participation as co-creator with God. "The problem of poverty then, is not primarily lack of material goods, but alienation from active participation in the community. Work is the activity through which men and women can find self-realization." Clearly, *On Human Work* sets a "priority of labor over capital."[5]

"Participation as an economic right is a comparatively new concept in social justice incorporated by the pastoral."[6] Participation has a basis in Scripture, as well as the tradition of the Catholic Church found in social encyclicals and the documents of Vatican II. The bishops' logic is this. Social justice is based on community. As a member, one is entitled by justice to participate in the community. A nation is a community. Every member is entitled to participate in the economy. Every member is entitled to employment.[7]

It is from these six moral principles and six recurring themes that a new vision of economic life is translated into concrete applications in specific areas of concern by the bishops.

Problems and Solutions

Despite strong pressure to drop policy proposals and "just teach general moral principles," the bishops chose four issues of concern and developed specific calls for legislative change. Among the "urgent problems" addressed are: unemployment, poverty, food and agriculture, and the U.S. economy and developing nations.

1. Area of Concern: Unemployment

Joblessness is becoming a more widespread and deep-seated problem in the U.S. The unemployment rate, often as high as seven percent since 1979, falls disproportionately on minorities and women. Unemployment denies participation in the productive life of the community; unemployment also has humanly destructive consequences ranging from a lowering of self-esteem to more serious social pathologies.

Solution: National commitment to full employment.

Work is good for humanity and for the individual, bringing both to fulfillment. "Production must be subordinated to the common good. This contradicts a materialistic view by emphasizing solidarity of all peoples and the evil of allowing anyone to be excluded from the economic activity of society." High employment levels are essential for overcoming the "ultimate injustice" of the marginalization process by which some persons are excluded from active participation in the human community.[8]

The economic pastoral says, "Full employment is the foundation of a just economy. . . . Employment is a basic right." To work is a right and a responsibility. One has a right to a wage that will sustain life in dignity. Human dignity makes workers privy to other rights that include rights to nondiscriminatory treatment, health care, old age disability insurance, healthy working conditions, rest and holidays, reasonable protection from arbitrary dismissal, notice of plant closings, and collective bargaining unionization. The greatest challenge of the bishops to U.S. managers is to foster greater labor-management cooperation. The longstanding antagonistic relationship between workers and employers will call for mutual trust and respect for each other's rights and responsibilities. Partnership between labor and management may include profit-sharing, employee stock ownership, and participatory decision making. Management needs to respect the role of unions; unions need to make "positive and creative contributions to the firm."

Other suggestions include business, labor, and government expanding on-the-job training programs and creating jobs to match the more than eight million Americans looking for work. New strategies need to be sought regarding time worked and pay received, and the economic conversion from a militarized economy to a peaceful and productive purpose. (#136-168, #298-304)[9]

2. Area of Concern: Poverty

One out of seven persons in the U.S. lives in poverty.[10] It is a problem distinct from unemployment. Many of the unemployed are not "poor" by official standards; many of the poor are not unemployed. The greatest number of the poor are children and women. Most of them are white, although a higher proportion of minorities lives in poverty.

The U.S. economy is marked by a very uneven distribution of wealth and income. The gap between rich and poor is growing and reflects an uneven allocation of power and opportunity as well as material goods. (#170-184)

Solution: Concerted effort to eradicate poverty. The bishops propose a shift in the distribution of wealth in the U.S. that would give a larger share to those below the poverty line. They agree that extreme inequities are detrimental to the development of social solidarity and community. Poverty in the economic sphere means that levels of power and participation are also uneven.

The bishops see the fulfillment of the basic needs of the poor as the highest priority because of human dignity and the preferential option for the poor. They call for solutions that respect the poor and enable them to take control of their own lives and to become self-sufficient through gainful employment. The perpetuating cycle of poverty, broken families, poor schools, crime, joblessness, and poor health can be broken.

The bishops make the following calls to action: take down the barriers to "full and equal employment for women and minorities;" foster self-help efforts to enable creative participation of the poor; restructure tax laws in light of the impact they have on the poor; establish national standards for minimum assistance and eligibility; reform welfare programs so that recipients receive adequate levels of assistance; evaluate assistance policies in light of their impact on the life and stability of the family; make a stronger commitment to education for the poor. (#188-215)

In calling for these solutions, the bishops are applying "distributive justice;" that is, that the government has a responsibility to see that the benefits and burdens of citizenship are allocated fairly.[11]

3. Area of Concern: Food and Agriculture

The U.S. food system is an integral part of the larger economy of the nation and the world.

In the diminishment of family farms and the increased concentration of land ownership, the bishops see a loss of a valued way of life of rural communities as well as the danger of large farm monopolies. Large agricultural operations tend to replace human labor with cheaper energy; to underpay farmworkers; and to use technologies that neglect soil and water conservation, spread pollution, and pose health hazards. (#220-230)

Solution: Protect Family Farms

The bishops make several calls for action: preserve family farms; protect the opportunity to take up farming as "a valuable form of work;" steward natural resources as central to agricultural policy." (#233-238)

The government, in their view, should legislate a progressive land tax to discourage excessively large land holdings; research ways of improving productivity of small and medium sized farms; insure just wages and benefits for farmworkers; and contribute to global food security. (#242- 250)

Contemporary economic practices have had a destructive impact on the environment. The economic pastoral calls those involved in agriculture and food production to solidarity and cooperation, and to see their participation as that of co-creators with God and stewards of the land they hold in trust for future generations.

4. Area of Concern: The U.S. Economy and Developing Nations

The non-industrialized nations suffer poverty that threatens health of body and degrades human decency. After startling statistics — "half the world's population lives in countries where the per capita annual income is

$400 or less" — the bishops present their view that the misery of the poor is the result of human decisions and human institutions. The inequalities between desperately poor countries and those with riches comes from the interaction and power of individual countries, and multi-national institutions or corporations intent on serving their own interests. There is a link between domestic and foreign issues. There has been a shift in national priorities from meeting human needs to promoting "national security." The U.S. spends 20 times more on defense than foreign aid. Assistance is too often dependent on our national relationship to a country and not on need. (#254-289)

Solution: Assist Poor Nations

The bishops endorse "a U.S. international economic policy designed to empower people everywhere and enable them to continue to develop a sense of their own worth, improve the quality of their lives, and ensure that the benefits of economic growth are shared equitably." (#292)

The U.S. has a moral obligation to help reduce world poverty. Policy issues called economic are moral. The impact of these policies on the poor and vulnerable of the world should be the criteria for judging their moral value.

There are interconnections and tradeoffs among competing interests and values. For example, lowering trade barriers affects jobs in the U.S. However, justice in wages and employment at home cannot be bought at the price of injustice on a global scale. Structural injustices, like global division of labor where profit is gained at another's expense, is unacceptable.

It is the development of the human person, not industrialization, that the bishops see as the model of "development." The Church's teaching on human dignity, the common good, the preferential option for the poor, and the whole range of rights — civil, political, social, and economic — is indeed a counter-perspective to what contemporary culture calls "development."

Reactions

Much public debate followed the publication of each of the three drafts of the economic pastoral.

Some alleged that the bishops did not understand the economic situation and thus overestimated the problem of marginalized population; that they did not grasp the reality of scarcity and risk-taking in an economy; and even underestimated the "consequences of social acts for the sinner."[12]

Some felt the bishops' proposals were nothing new, just a plea for more spending on programs that have not lessened poverty over the past decades.

Others felt the bishops had done their homework but had come to the wrong conclusions. They felt that the bishops were threatening the capitalistic system. Their critiques focused on the increased role of government the pastoral proposes.

Some affirmative commentaries saw the pastoral as really about "the conflict between faith and culture." American culture fosters materialism and considers economic accomplishments as indicators of human worth. Faith holds that anything less than God can become an idol and that persons must be valued over things. One professor of social ethics wrote: "A country where some can get rich is not a country where all can get rich; a country where people are prompted above all by the desire to get rich is a morally poor one."[13]

The bishops raise the issue of the uneasy fit between Christian faith and the current American economy. The dilemma the document never wrestles with is whether the prosperity of the industrialized world may be incompatible with the notions of human fulfillment and virtuous living.

Questioning the current cultural attitude about the economy was so alarming to some conservative Catholics that even before the bishops' pastoral was published, William Simon and Michael Novak issued a letter which they called *Toward the Future*. They see the American free enterprise system, even as it is, as the most respectful of individual freedom and welfare. They believe that American self-interest is likely to be strong enough to work for the good of the society.[14]

There is nothing wrong with the system, Simon and Novak contend. "The problem is with persons who fail to use the liberties afforded by this system wisely and well."[15] "A free society should not be blamed for the results attained by some free citizens. The American system of opportunity to go as far as one's talents take one is the only moral system worthy of a free people."[16]

Andrew Greeley, sociologist and journalist, calls the bishops' pastoral a failure because it deals with symptoms instead of root causes. The letter "does not address the most fundamental problem of the American economy, excessive size and unjustifiable concentration of power, which is the most serious cause of both poverty and unemployment."[17]

Another critic calls the letter a "Pastoral for the Poor." The bishops do not consider that their proposals will "burden the economy with more government intervention and spending. The growing cost of entitlements to antipoverty programs and Social Security is already the biggest obstacle to eliminating the budget deficit."[18] Because responsibilities and obligations have not been spelled out by the bishops along with rights, "one could imagine a just country providing for the welfare of the least advantaged and at once being unjust because of the way resulting costs were placed on the rest of the population."[19]

The bishops, however, see the contemporary situation as worsening and reject the notion that the poor will be helped by the capitalist market system. "The bishops' critique of capitalism is that the root of the problem is in institutional patterns and power relationships which enable certain persons, as opposed to others, to participate more actively and powerfully in economic life. Capitalism is built on essential antagonistic class interests. Full employment is not attainable because regulated levels of unemployment benefit capital by increasing their political and economic power over labor who compete for scarce jobs." Welfare and unemployment compensation are potentially dangerous because they encourage people to stay as they are.

The bishops' proposal for economic democracy and economic planning may be one solution to the problem of monopoly capital and marginalization. However, in calling for more government intervention and affirming private property and initiative in the marketplace, the bishops seem more fearful of "threats to social democracy than to the actual marginalizing effects of private monopoly capital."[20]

The bishops argue that market forces have not and will not solve many of the problems faced in today's economy and that cooperation rather than competition should be sought as a means of restoring social justice.

This fact may have led to the bishops' proposals asking for government intervention. This was disconcerting to some people. The bishops, however, see government as a positive instrument of the community and understand that "the moral claims for political democracy are other than and deeper than the moral claims for capitalism."[21] The bishops reaffirm the "Catholic understanding of government as middle ground between individualism and collectivism," and reject a "statist" position. The purpose of the state is the common good, and the common good does not deny the basic rights of the individual. The state exists as a help for individuals and associations. The economic pastoral "emphasizes participation of the individual in the total life of the community as a right based on social justice with a corresponding duty of society and all others to recognize and facilitate this right."[22]

Government is to "coordinate and regulate diverse groups in society in a way that leads to the common good and protection of basic rights." Not only government should function in this way, but industry, schools, the arts, even the family.[23] "The bishops propose a reforming approach rejecting a radical destruction of the existing economic system, but they also call for many modifications within the system to overcome the individualistic emphasis that is often present today."[24] The criticism in the pastoral is not directed so much at an economic system as against an ethical and cultural system that has come to ignore ethical and religious dimensions.

Conclusion

The American Catholic Bishops' economic pastoral points out problems with the U.S. economy. It calls for actions that respect the dignity of each person and his or her right to economic participation. Although the bishops were accused of not understanding the economy, Nobel laureate in economics James Tobin affirms many of their proposals to curb poverty and unemployment.[25] Businesses have shown productivity increases when there is increased recognition of the role and treatment of employees.[26] Perhaps others will find wisdom in the bishops' words and ideas. Answering this timely call could mean economic justice for all.

Endnotes

[1]*Economic Justice for All: Pastoral Letter on Catholic Social Teaching and the U.S. Economy.* Washington, D.C.: National Conference of Catholic Bishops, 1986. Further citations are by paragraph number.

[2]Stephen Brickham, "The Bishops' Pastoral: A Theory of Justice," *Journal of Business Ethics*, Vol.7, No. 6 (June 1988), p. 439. James E. Hug, "Measuring the Shock Waves: the Economic Pastoral," *New Catholic World*, Vol. 229, No. 1373 (September/October 1986), p. 212.

[3]Bruce Douglas, "At the Heart of the Letter," *Commonweal*, Vol. 112, No. 12 (June 1985). John J. LaFalce, "Catholic Social Teaching and Economic Justice," *America*, Vol. 152 (May 1985).

[4]For further background see "Preferential Option: Language and Meaning," *America*, Vol. 153 (September 1985).

[5]Brien Hallett, "Pope John Paul II's Challenge to the American Bishops," *America*, Vol. 152 (May 1985), pp. 371-374.

[6]Charles E. Curran, "Ethical Principles of Catholic Social Teaching Behind the United States Bishops' Letter on the Economy," *Journal of Business Ethics*, vol.7, no. 6, June 1988, p. 415.

[7]For further scriptural development of "participation" see Brickham, p. 440.

[8]Richard P. Mullin, "The Work Ethic of the Bishops' Pastoral Letter on the Economy," *Journal of Business Ethics*, Vol.7, No. 6 (June 1988), pp. 422-424.

[9]Robert L. Armacost, "Productivity and the Economic Pastoral: Implications for Growth," *Journal of Business Ethics*, Vol.7, No. 6 (June 1988), p. 471. See also in the same journal Daniel J. Koys, "Values Underlying Personnel/Human Resource Management: Implications of the Bishops' Economic Pastoral Letter."

[10]According to the U.S. Census Bureau, 33.6 million Americans lived in poverty in 1990. The so-called "poverty line" for a family of four was $13,359. *St. Petersburg Times*, September 27, 1991.

[11]Curran, p. 415.

[12]See, for example, James P. Egan, "Sin and the Economic Analysis of the Pastoral: A Class Act?" *Journal of Business Ethics*, Vol. 7, No. 6 (June 1988).

[13]J. Philip Wogaman, "The Great Economic Debate Continues," *Journal of Ecumenical Studies*, Vol. 24, No. 3 (Summer 1987), p. 419. See also articles previously cited by Douglas and Mullin, as well as Peter Steinfels, "From Adam Smith to the American Catholic Bishops: Debating Visions of Economic Life," *Journal of Business Ethics*, Vol. 7, No. 6 (June 1988).

[14]Michael Novak and William Simon, eds., *Toward the Future*, Lay Commission on Catholic Social Teaching and the U.S. Economy, 1984, pp. 24, 50f.

[15]*Ibid.*, p. 35.

[16]Michael Novak, "Where the Second Draft Errs," *America*, Vol. 154 (January 1986), p. 24.

[17]Andrew M. Greeley, "The Bishops and the Economy: A 'Radical' Dissent," *America*, Vol. 152 (January 1985), p. 24.

[18]Edward L. Hennessy, "A Pastoral for the Poor, Not the Economy," *America*, Vol. 152 (January 1985), p. 15.

[19]Douglas, p. 362.

[20]Christopher L. Pines, "The Bishops' Dilemma with Capitalism: A Critical Analysis," *Journal of Business Ethics*, Vol. 7, No. 6 (June 1988), pp. 445-447, 450.

[21]Wogaman, pp. 526f.

[22]Curran, pp. 413-416.

[23]Douglas, p. 360.

[24]Curran, p. 417.

[25]James Tobin, "Unemployment, Poverty and Economic Policy," *America*, Vol. 152 (May 1985), p. 359.

[26]Armacost, p. 472 and Brickham, p. 442.

Charles Lewis Fisk Jr.

Economic Justice for All in a Capitalist Economy?

In November of 1986 the National Conference of Catholic Bishops published *Economic Justice for All: Pastoral Letter on Catholic Social Teaching and the U.S. Economy.* The main thrust of the letter is to focus attention on the human and ethical aspects of economic life in the United States.

An exploration of these issues requires some understanding of the fundamental nature of the American economic system: capitalism and its dimensions.

This system evolved in Europe out of the gradual breakdown of the forces of political authority and tradition, the two powerful mechanisms which had brought order to economic life. By the late eighteenth century capitalism had emerged. In *The Wealth Of Nations* (1776), Adam Smith became the first to describe its internal workings.

As the Industrial Revolution continued throughout the nineteenth century, technological innovation and large-scale manufacturing produced a dramatic population shift out of agriculture and into the factory. As industrial employment increased, attention came to be focused on the wages and conditions of workers.

In his 1891 encyclical *Rerum Novarum* ("On The Condition Of Working People") Pope Leo XIII spelled out the position of the Catholic Church on these issues. Though he embraced the concept of private property, Pope Leo would not sanction the "commodification" of labor, the buying and selling of workers at a market-determined wage. Instead, the Pope endorsed the concept of a "just wage."

Rerum Novarum did not alter the process by which labor was allocated and remunerated. It did, however, ally the Catholic Church with the movement to reform capitalism.

On May 1, 1991, the centennial of *Rerum Novarum*, Pope John Paul II echoed these sentiments in his ninth encyclical *Centesimus Annus* ("The 100th Year").[1] He endorsed capitalism as "an economic system which recognizes the fundamental and positive role of business, the market, private property and the resulting responsibility for the means of production as well as human creativity in the economic sector." (#42) Moreover, he noted that the Catholic Church "acknowledges the legitimate role of profit." (#35)

However, the pope recognized drawbacks associated with the profit motive:

> Alienation is found also in work, when it is organized so as to ensure maximum returns and profits with no concern whether the worker, through his own labor, grows or diminishes as a person, either through increased sharing in a genuinely supportive community or through increased isolation in a maze of relationships marked by destructive competitiveness and estrangement, in which he is considered only a means and not an end. (#41)

While displaying an awareness of capitalism's darker side, *Centesimus Annus* gives sanction to capitalism as a legitimate system for organizing the economic life of society. Inherent within capitalism are several dimensions — economic, social, and moral — which must be considered for an understanding of the pastoral letter on the U.S. economy.

The Dimensions of Capitalism

Capitalism is generally defined as an economic system which utilizes the market mechanism — the interaction of supply and demand — to determine what products and services will be produced, how they will be produced, and how they will be distributed throughout society.

Necessary for this process is the establishment of a system of property rights to create and support private ownership of the resources needed for production. Economists classify these resources as land, labor and capital. These three "factors of production" are purchased in markets. The prices paid for each are defined as rents, wages, and interest, respectively. These payments represent production costs to business enterprises. The difference between these costs and the money that can be obtained by selling the resulting output is identified as profit.

The concept of profit — and loss — is inseparable from a capitalist economy. Profit is the driving force within the system.

It is the endless pursuit of profit that sustains a capitalist economy. Economists from Adam Smith to Karl Marx to the present have grappled with the concept of profit, and in the process have generated a variety of explanations regarding the origin of profit within the system.

Profit not only does exist, but must exist in a capitalistic system. Profit is a source of wealth. When the ownership and control of wealth is concentrated, so also will be the flow of profit. Therefore, a substantial inequality in the distribution of wealth is inevitable within a capitalist economy. In *The Wealth of Nations* Adam Smith observed: "Whenever there is great prosperity, there is great inequality. For one very rich man, there must be at least five hundred poor, and the affluence of the rich supposes the indigence of the many."[2]

Some recent data should serve to put this issue into more concrete terms. By the early 1980s the share of wealth owned by the top one-half of 1 percent of U.S. households was approximately 27 percent; that of the top 10 percent of households was approximately 68 percent.[3]

Another dimension of capitalism, both economic and social, involves the relationship between owners of capital and the workers who supply the needed labor for production. Owners and workers are united by the market.[4]

On the surface, utilization of the market process might seem to place owners and workers on an equal footing. Producers who own the plant and equipment have the right to offer or withhold jobs, but workers have the right to offer or withhold their ability to work.

But implicit in this relationship is a system of domination stemming from the indisputably unequal degree of power held by each of the participants – owners and workers – in the labor market. Products are not owned by the workers who produce them; they belong to those who own factories and machines and employ labor.

Employers, through the ability and right to withhold employment are clearly dominant in this nexus. Only if workers have reasonably good alternative employment opportunities would there exist an equal sharing of power.

One additional dimension of capitalism is the issue of morality. In their pastoral letter, the bishops apply "basic moral principles" to their evaluation of the U.S. economy. In a very real sense, capitalism can be considered to have its own innate morality.[5]

Acquisitiveness — more crudely stated, greed — lies at the very core of capitalism. The ceaseless search for more profit to invest in more capital to produce more goods that can be sold for even more profit is the driving force that sustains capitalism. Reconciling this with the Scriptures' condemnation of acquisitiveness and the amassing of wealth was no small problem for early expositors of capitalism, Adam Smith included.

While being quite aware of the moral costs associated with the acquisition of wealth, Smith resolved the issue for himself by maintaining that the material benefits outweighed the moral costs. As noted economist and social analyst Robert Heilbroner explains it, "whatever served the individual served society:"

> By logical analogy, whatever created a profit (and thereby served the individual capitalist) also served society, so that a blanket moral exemption was, so to speak, extended over the entire range of activity that passed the profit-and-loss test of the marketplace. . . . Thus a kind of moral pardon is applied to all licit activities of the capital accumulating sector.[6]

The claim is often made that capitalism is amoral; no judgement of right or wrong accompanies the workings of the market. But an argument can be made that there is indeed a morality inherent within the market system. Any legal activity which passes the profit test is "good." Acquisitiveness is not only condoned but rewarded. Equity, the issue of fairness, has no place in the profit-maximizing process.

However, these very social and moral dimensions of capitalism were the issues which the American Catholic Bishops set out to address.

Economic Justice For All: The Pastoral Letter

"We speak as moral teachers, not economic technicians," the bishops state in their introductory comment. "We seek not to make some political or ideological point but to lift up the human and ethical dimensions of economic life, aspects too often neglected in public discussion."[7] The bishops maintain as a central point that certain basic economic rights apply to all human beings. These include a right to food, clothing, shelter, education, rest, medical care, and employment.

Those who wish to move society toward any specific goal, must do so with an awareness of both the possibilities and the limitations dictated by the framework of the economic system. Is the bishops' program practical?

Employment

The economic issue that emerges from the pastoral letter as being the most critical is employment. It is inextricably linked to the other economic rights enumerated by the bishops. It is the primary determinant of access to food, clothing, shelter, education, rest, and medical care for most people.

The bishops contend that "work with adequate pay for all who seek it is the primary means for achieving basic justice in our society." (#73) Is full employment achievable in the United States? The issue is complex.

First, there is the conceptual problem of determining precisely what "full employment" means. In the U.S. this problem is approached from the reverse; that is, the level of unemployment is calculated and a goal is established for the unemployment rate. Full employment is then considered to be some "acceptable" rate on unemployment.

Unemployment is subdivided into various categories based on the particular circumstances causing potential workers to be without jobs. These circumstances include:

the seasonality of the occupation; the voluntarily shifting from one job to another; the displacement of workers brought about by industry restructuring and technological change; the lack of appropriate education or training for available jobs; age, gender and race discrimination; and, finally, the recessionary phase of the business cycle: the recurring upswings and downswings in business activity which are innate in capitalism.

The official "unemployment rate," determined by the Bureau of Labor Statistics, is the percentage of the "labor force" which is without jobs but actively seeking work. The bureau's calculation of the size of the labor force causes the official rate to understate the true degree of unemployment in the United States. This understatement occurs for two reasons. First, discouraged potential workers who, out of sheer frustration or despair, have stopped "actively looking" for work are not counted as part of the labor force. And second, no distinction is made between part-time and full-time employment. Part-time workers who would prefer full-time work if it were available are, in a true economic sense, partly unemployed. However, they receive the same classification as do fully employed workers.

With an awareness of these measurement problems, what unemployment rate would be consistent with the goal of full employment set forth by the bishops? Certainly not zero percent; seasonal occupations and voluntary movement by workers from job to job would be normal even in a fully employed economy. What is it then?

Although the bishops do not identify in their letter any specific unemployment rate which they believe would be consistent with the goal of full employment, they do provide some indication of what they think it might be:

Several areas of U.S. economic life demand special attention. Unemployment is the most basic.
... Over the past two decades the nation has come
to tolerate an increasing level of unemployment.
The 6 to 7 percent deemed acceptable today
would have been intolerable twenty years ago.
(#15)

Twenty years prior to the publication of this letter the
unemployment rate was less than four percent. During
World War II it was less than two percent. Even during
the economic expansion of the mid-to-late 1980s, the
lowest level to which the unemployment rate declined to
was about six percent. By March of 1992, with another
recession in progress, it stood at 7.3 percent.

Though no specific unemployment rate is targeted in
the letter, the bishops clearly imply a goal well below the
rates of recent years.

Why has full employment been so elusive? The answer
lies embedded within the economic system. Full employment, as it is understood by the bishops, is in conflict with
the driving force of capitalism: the quest for profit.

One source of conflict stems from the fact that higher
wages tend to squeeze producers' profit margins. The
closer the economy approaches true full employment, the
tighter labor markets become. That is, the pool of available workers begins to dry up. As a result, labor costs tend
to rise as workers are able to translate their enhanced
power in the market into higher wages and better working
conditions. The existence of a pool of unemployed
workers functions like a pressure valve to prevent wages
from rising. Some substantial degree of unemployment,
therefore, is beneficial to business firms in their drive for
profits.

If this perspective seems somewhat extreme, consider this excerpt taken from a mainstream college-level economics text:

> Some economists view the possibility of widespread layoffs as a curb to excessive demands for wages and fringe benefits. Threats of unemployment may also reduce "goldbricking" and may be good work incentives for people who respond better to "sticks" than to "carrots." These are the *"disciplinary benefits"* to firms (and consumers) from having some slack in labor markets.[8]

This statement is blatantly indicative of an owner's dominance over his workers. Merely the threat of losing their jobs constrains workers from seeking higher wages or improved working conditions. The availability of unemployed labor makes the threat viable.

On the other hand, while some degree of unemployment is beneficial to the drive for profits, clearly, too much unemployment upsets the process. Any decline in workers' incomes reduces the market demand for goods and services, which then causes profits to decline. The process of capitalist expansion has always been characterized by an unevenness which, in contemporary jargon, is referred to as the business cycle, consisting of its alternating phases of expansion and contraction.

The greatest contraction occurred during the Great Depression. The unemployment rate peaked at nearly 25 percent in 1933; business spending for new plant and equipment almost disappeared for a time. The outbreak of World War II brought a dramatic change. Fueled by massive government wartime spending in the industrialized countries, economic recovery followed.

In the post-war period government's expanded role in the economy continued. Government spending provided the boost necessary to prevent another economic crisis of the magnitude of the Great Depression. And clearly this purpose has been served; recessions in the United States in the post-war period have been much less severe than during the pre-war period.

But this commitment on the part of government to support the level of spending in the economy creates an inflationary bias. Producers are more apt to increase prices when they anticipate strong consumer demand. At some point, however, as inflation worsens, the market process becomes disrupted and the profit seeking process is threatened. The usual solution to this problem in the U.S. is to have the Federal Reserve (the central bank) limit the amount of money and credit available. The resulting decline in spending eventually leads to economic recession.

Inducing a recession is a very effective means of slowing inflation. But only at the cost of a rising unemployment rate. This trade-off between inflation and unemployment is another major obstacle in the road to full employment. Any effort to move aggressively to reduce unemployment much below its current level would be interpreted as likely to cause an unacceptable increase in the rate of inflation.

An alternative solution, one consistent with full employment, does exist. Price stability can be achieved by limiting the total income earned by owners and workers to an amount equal to the total value of all the goods and services produced. This approach would require specific government policies designed to control money flows such as wages, prices, and profits. This would preclude having to orchestrate a recession — with its vastly disproportionate burdens — as a remedy for inflation.

What are the prospects, then, for achieving full employment in the United States? If full employment is interpreted to mean a reasonable access to a job for anyone who desires one, then the prospects, in the near term anyway, are not very good.

The policies that would be required to keep inflation in check, in an economy with real full employment, would limit the degree of freedom that business firms and workers (through professional associations as well as labor unions) would have in the market; they would lose some of their control over prices and wages. These powerful interest groups would have to yield some of their power to government. The political consensus necessary to support this alternative — present to a varying extent in Japan and some western European countries — is not present in the United States today.

Those who have a real concern about trying to alleviate the hardships of unemployment in America will have to settle, in the short run at least, for band-aid solutions. Support can be marshalled for programs that provide education and training to the unemployed. Political pressure can be aimed at providing unemployment benefits which are consistent with a minimum acceptable standard of living. Social services can be provided to help people deal with the adverse psychological and social impacts of unemployment.

These types of measures, however, do not solve the problem of an insufficient number of jobs. A long-term solution requires a political consensus to make a real commitment to full employment. Advocates must work toward increasing public awareness of both the scope and severity of the problem.

Wages

A second focus of the pastoral — one closely related to employment — is the issue of wages. The bishops state: "Millions are poor because they have lost their jobs or because their wages are too low." (#196) The working poor are those who are employed but earn incomes which are too low to provide some minimum standard of living. This phenomenon is a natural result of the normal functioning of the market.

Capitalism's endless search for profit has been identified as its most salient feature. The maximization of profit requires that producers minimize their costs of production. Wages account for approximately three quarters of total production costs in the United States. Producers have a vested interest, therefore, in paying the lowest wage possible for the labor needed for production.

The relative power of employers and employees in determining wages is vastly unequal. Producers, who own the means of production and control the access to jobs, dominate. In an economy which rarely ever approaches what would be, from a progressive perspective, real full employment, the dominant position of the owner over the worker results in a lower wage than that which would result if power were shared equally.

One avenue available to labor to counterbalance the market power of employers is the right to organize. Labor's right to do so was first recognized by the Catholic Church in *Rerum Novarum* (1891). In those sectors of the American economy where workers have been well organized, wages have been improved. But this has come largely at the expense of nonunionized labor. And unionized workers are in the minority, representing less than twenty percent of the American labor force today.

Other factors have contributed to the low-wage problem in the United States. Mergers of already large corporations bring about restructurings that eliminate many jobs and thereby increase the pool of unemployed labor. Capital flight to low-wage countries, the relative growth of the service sector with its low-paying jobs, job discrimination, employers' increasing propensity to hire part-time workers — all of these have worsened conditions in the market for labor.

The only effective solution to the wage problem is a commitment to full employment. This commitment does not appear to be close at hand. The immediate outlook for labor in the United States is, therefore, not very promising.

Medical Care and Housing

The pastoral letter also recognizes access to medical care and housing to be fundamental human rights. Unemployment and inadequate wages for many people restrict their access to these necessities. In the absence of full employment and adequate wages, there are only two alternatives for providing everyone with adequate medical care and housing. Either government must directly undertake their production and distribution, or it must provide people with the money needed to purchase them.

The bishops cite Pope John Paul II's 1981 encyclical *Laborem Exercens* ("On Human Work") as an endorsement of governmental activism under the "principle of socialization." However, given the generally anti-government sentiment permeating American society today, creating the political consensus needed to effect the socialization of the production of medical care and housing will be a difficult task.

A more feasible alternative appears to be that which combines government funding with private production.

But reasonable access to medical care and housing will not occur without a political consensus to support a substantially increased role for government.

Housing and medical care must be thought of as public goods. Their provision and distribution can not be left to the workings of an unfettered market. In one way or another, government must be an active participant in these markets.

Morality

Finally, what can be said about the issue of morality? The pastoral letter presents a moral vision for economic life in American society. The bishops contend that economic decisions are subject to moral scrutiny:

> Investment and management decisions have crucial moral dimensions: they create jobs or eliminate them; they can push vulnerable families over the edge into poverty or give them new hope for the future; they help or hinder the building of a more equitable society. (#92)

Capitalism has an innate moral dimension. Any licit activity that is profitable receives the sanction of the marketplace. Production that generates profit is legitimized by virtue of its own profitability.

By extension, any decisions made by business firms to maximize profits are legitimized. When decisions are made regarding plant closings or relocations, corporate mergers and restructurings, acquisitions of new labor-saving technology and the like, capitalism provides producers immunity from having to concern themselves with any social and economic hardships which befall human beings as a result of profit maximizing decisions.

The market process does not and can not address the issue of equity. When corporate executives make a decision that improves productive efficiency, the decision is, *ipso facto,* good. Whether or not some workers are harmed by the decision is a question which the market is absolved from having to answer.

It is in this moral dimension that the basic principles laid out by the bishops are in greatest conflict with capitalism. The dignity of the human person is not a consideration in the making of profit maximizing decisions. Willingness and ability to work will not guarantee employment. The poor and the vulnerable are of little consequence in the market. The moral vision of the pastoral letter will not be a natural outgrowth of capitalism.

Conclusion

Capitalism's greatest attribute is its historically un-rivalled capacity to produce goods and services. The material abundance which the system can generate is almost overwhelming. Total production in the United States today is more than sufficient to provide all Americans with an adequate standard of living. However, extreme inequality and a significant degree of instability are also inherent within capitalism. Economic justice as envisioned in the pastoral letter will not be a natural outgrowth of capitalism.

Ironically, capitalism also provides the possibility for society to move in the direction of economic justice. Because capitalism is consistent with a significant degree of political freedom, the potential exists for society, through its political institutions, to modify the natural results of the unfettered market.

Creating the political support needed to effect change will be difficult. Public attention must be turned toward the issue of economic justice. Perceptions that any government involvement in the economy is necessarily inefficient or wasteful must be altered. The issue of equity must be brought to the forefront when deciding who will benefit from government action.

Those intending to pursue the vision of economic justice set forth in the pastoral letter must do so with a keen awareness of economic reality. Capitalism can generate a vast outpouring of goods to satisfy society's material desires. But economic justice will not, indeed cannot, occur as the automatic by-product of a capitalist economy. The moral question regarding the just or fair distribution of capitalist production must be answered in the political arena, not in the market. It is to the political process that society must turn if economic justice is to prevail.

Endnotes

[1]Pope John Paul II, *Centesimus Annus*, in *National Catholic Reporter*, May 24, 1991. Citations are by paragraph number.

[2]Adam Smith, *The Wealth of Nations*, Oxford: Clarendon Press, 1976, pp. 709-710.

[3]Kevin Phillips, *The Politics Of Rich And Poor*, New York: Random House, 1990, p. 11.

[4]Robert L. Heilboner, *The Nature and Logic of Capitalism*, New York: Norton, 1985, pp. 65-69. This book presents a sophisticated but highly readable exploration of capitalism.

[5]*Ibid.*, pp. 112-116.

[6]*Ibid.*, pp. 115-116.

[7]National Conference of Catholic Bishops, *Economic Justice For All: Pastoral Letter on Catholic Social Teaching and the U.S. Economy*, Washington, D.C.: United States Catholic Conference, 1986, p. vii. Further citations are by paragraph number.

[8]Ralph T. Byrns and Gerald W. Stone, *Macroeconomics*, Glenville, Ill.: Scott Foresman & Company, 1989, p. 108.

Partners in the Mystery of Redemption: A Pastoral Response to Women's Concerns for Church and Society (1988)

Excerpted by Jeanine Jacob

The diversity among Catholic women contradicts the claim that there is a typical Catholic woman, easily defined and understood, whose needs and wants are readily identifiable. Catholic women are extremely diverse in their concerns, yet in this diversity common themes do appear. (#12)

In a world fraught with moral confusion, women want the church to proclaim clearly and consistently its teachings on the value and dignity of the human person. Women have talents and gifts to offer church and society, and they want to use them. They want to be heard and consulted as members of the body of Christ. Both their dignity as persons and the good of the church demand such recognition. (#13)

Sexist attitudes and behavior discriminate against persons solely because they are female or male. Historically, women have borne the brunt of this prejudice. . . . Sexism, as many women said, creates barriers to communication. It hampers collaboration and contributes to pornography, violence and prostitution. The sin of sexism depersonalizes women. It makes them objects to be possessed and used. It degrades dignity. It dismisses women as unimportant, as mere subordinates or appendages. (#28)

In the face of such debasement, women challenge the church not only to express in words its support of their dignity, but to take the lead in actions that accord them the respect they deserve. (#29)

"When anyone believes that men are inherently superior to women or that women are inherently superior to men, then he or she is guilty of sexism. Sexism is a moral and social evil." [Bishops Victor Balke and Raymond Lucker, "Male and Female God Created Them"] (#39)

Acknowledging the subtle presence of sexism and affirming the equality and dignity of women is only a first step. We must and do pledge to reject clearly and consistently human structures and patterns of activity that in any way treat women of lesser worth than men. When our actions do not conform to our ideals, all suffer. We therefore regret and confess our individual and collective failures to respond to women as they deserve. (#41)

"Society gives women a double message. On the one hand they are valued for their childbearing and nurturing capabilities. But contemporary society also makes them feel somehow insufficient unless they hold degrees and can pursue professional jobs." (Fort Leavenworth Catholic Chapel, Kan.) (#48)

At the heart of loving relationships between women and men, there is an element of freedom and responsibility that distinguishes human sexuality from any form of sex in lower levels of life. Human love at its best has been likened to the outpouring of God's love. Sex isolated from love can lead even in marriage to violence and sin, destroying relationships and mutual self-esteem and creating a terrible loneliness. (#100)

The mutual love of Catholic couples should be open to bearing new life. Married lovers, who freely become life-givers, respond to God in an act of other-centered fidelity and service. Marriage is ordered not only toward unitive love and procreation of children but also toward the establishment of a community in which they may be reared. (#101)

We believe the family will only be strengthened to the degree that husbands and wives become partners in parenting. If the family "is to achieve the full flowering of its life and mission, it needs the kindly communion of minds and the joint deliberation of spouses as well as the painstaking cooperation of parents in the education of their children." [Second Vatican Council, *Gaudium et Spes*, 52] The children of single parents may need additional pastoral care, which the church in part can offer through its family services. (#113)

While the church honors women as wives and mothers and highly values their work in the home, it accords full honor and dignity to lay women and religious who remain single and creatively express their commitments in ministry and service. However, the presence of single women in the church has to become more visible in parishes and support groups. They should receive more encouragement and signs of appreciation for the depth of their intimacy with God and their ministry to other people. (#115)

We pledge to offer compassionate assistance to all women — young women, women who have never married and those who are preparing for marriage, women already married and those who are struggling with separation, divorce, homosexuality or the death of a spouse. Lesbian women deserve special understanding and support from the Christian community to enable them to live a chaste and loving celibate life. At the same time, we must be ready to hear, with pastoral solicitude and concern, what these women have to say about the particular ways in which their dignity as women is belittled and demeaned by sexism abetted by cultural prejudices. Attentive care must especially be offered to women and men who have contracted diseases that are sexually transmitted and can be life threatening. In these and in all cases, human beings merit compassion, understanding and solicitous counsel. (#126)

It is an unfortunate reality in our era that the eucharistic celebration, the supreme source of unity, has become for some an occasion of divisiveness, pain and frustration. Some women refuse to participate in the liturgy because it is presided over by men only. (#201)

As bishops, we do not wish to ignore the genuine aspirations of women to be included more in the church's liturgical, administrative and pastoral life. (#202)

Continuing reflection, dialogue and even controversy in regard to the ordination of women demonstrate the value of further study in order to deepen our understanding of the relationship of this question to Christian anthropology, the sacrament of holy orders and ministry in the church. (#219)

[W]e recommend that women participate in all liturgical ministries that do not require ordination. (#222)

Having written these words, we must see to it that the church, on the national, diocesan and parochial level, enables this letter to come to life. The dialogue between women and men must continue to be expanded so that our recommendations become part of the living heritage of our Catholic people and our institutions. Implementation is essential, for ours must not be a counterfeit love of formal politeness, impersonal tolerance or empty words. (#246)

Note: This first published draft was susperseded by subsequent pastoral drafts in 1989 and 1992.

Jude Michael Ryan

Women and the Catholic Church: The Bishops' Perspective

The American Catholic Bishops' draft pastoral letter on the concerns of women was published in 1988. Entitled *Partners in the Mystery of Redemption: A Pastoral Response to Women's Concerns for Church and Society,* it is broadly divided into four chapters: "Partners in Personhood," "Partners in Relationships," "Partners in Society," and "Partners in the Church."

The justification for the bishops' letter is summed up in their own words:

> First, the pastoral is a *report* on what we have heard. Second it is a *reflection* on our heritage. Third it is a *response* intended to show that we have listened to women's voices and taken them seriously, that we seek to remedy the injustices women denounce and to promote the positive values they advocate.[1]

The letter has been widely circulated during the course of several revisions as the bishops sought input from diverse groups of people. Despite this broad-based approach, the pastoral has not been produced without controversy. Some who have read the letter feel that it goes too far in embracing ideas which are not part of Church tradition, while others believe the document does not go far enough in this direction.

Overview

The first section of the proposed pastoral, "Partners in Personhood," addresses the need for recognition of equality between the sexes. Prior to the Second Vatican Council (1962-1965), the pastoral points out, official Church teaching did not adequately address the concerns of women. Since that time, Popes John XXIII, Paul VI, and John Paul II have spoken out against sexism and supported the notion that women are in all ways equal to men. "Women and men, by virtue of their baptism," say the bishops, "are reborn in Christ and are, therefore, intended for equal partnership in celebration of their mutuality and uniqueness before God." (#35)

The bishops make three important points in this section of the letter. The first is to recognize that the Church has a long history of sexist attitudes and behaviors:

> As we ponder the profound truth and saving grace of our baptism in Christ and our membership in the Church, we are called to recognize that sexist attitudes have also colored church teaching and practice over the centuries and still in our day. (#39)

This is supported by the testimony of some women who reported that they were advised by their priests to offer their suffering up to God when trying to get help in dealing with abusive husbands. (#40)

The second point is that sexism is morally unacceptable behavior. "The sin of sexism depersonalizes women. It makes them objects to be possessed and used. It degrades dignity. It dismisses women as unimportant, as mere subordinates or appendages." (#28) Identifying sexism as "sin" strengthens the argument that such attitudes are inconsistent with the values and standards of the Church.

Thirdly, the bishops take the view that men and women play different roles in life, but they underscore that one gender is not inferior to the other because of these distinctive roles. This position is developed in the subsequent chapter, "Partners in Relationships."

While men and women are considered equals, the role of women in marriage and child-rearing is acknowledged as having been historically different from that of men. The bishops urge greater involvement on the part of fathers in the raising of children. This, the bishops argue, will strengthen the family unit and assure its continuity as the single most important institution in American life. The bishops see themselves as "countercultural" in arguing for a strong family and marital fidelity in light of the many societal pressures which seem to urge family disintegration and sexual promiscuity. It is this subject of human sexuality which most occupies the bishops in this chapter. They cite Pope Paul VI's 1968 encyclical *Humanae Vitae*: "The encyclical opposes any form of casual sex or artificial contraception. It defends the well-being of women, fidelity, feminine dignity and the right to life." (#55)

It is this specific area of artificial contraception which seems to cause great concern for both the Church hierarchy and the laity, due in large part to the fact that many women ignore the Church's teachings in this area.

> A challenging reality of our time, according to the testimony of women and available statistics, is that there is a wide gap between what the Church teaches about artificial contraception and the actual practice of many Catholic women. (#73)

The evidence is provided by a 1982 study of American women by the National Center of Health Statistics, which shows that there is no relationship between women's religious affiliations and the use of artificial contraceptives. (#74) This evidence suggests that Catholic women are no more likely to refrain from the use of artificial contraceptives than are women of any other religious faith or of no particular religious faith. While the first chapter looked to men to alter their attitudes and behaviors regarding women, the second chapter urges the Church to examine itself regarding this challenge and better educate Catholics in an effort to demonstrate a link between healthy human relationships and God's grace.

But more may be needed. According to Archbishop Rembert Weakland of Milwaukee, human sexuality is one of the most important issues challenging the Church today.

> Sexuality — that's the big one. We haven't come to terms with it at all. Our scientific understanding is still rudimentary. Normal sexual drives, homosexuality, pedophilia. Contraception — the fact that science can control or modify human reproduction. It is a great and frightening frontier, the Galileo issue of our day. And the Church is reluctant to accept the results of the human sciences; instead, it harks back to the days when you could say, "This is black, this is white; this right, this wrong." [2]

The bishops also address in this chapter those persons who feel alienated from the Church because they do not find themselves in the kind of family structures traditionally defined by the Church. Both single women and those identifying themselves as lesbians seem to feel most alienated:

> There is emerging a new class of single people to which the church must pay more attention. Yet

despite this statistical increase, many single
women point out that there is in the church a
noticeable lack of consistent, competent pastoral
care for persons who are unmarried, separated,
divorced or widowed. (#70)

The third chapter of the letter, "Partners in Society,"
broadens the scope of the essay from dealing with the
Church and its members to the overall attitude of society
toward half its membership. This chapter attempts to
reconcile current Church teachings with society's general
attitudes toward women. "Many women detect in our
culture a pervasive sexist bias, directly opposed to basic
justice," the bishops write. (#135)

These injustices can be found in the home, as one
Florida woman reported: ". . . people say about housework
that it isn't real work. Sometimes women themselves feel
that way. They say, 'I don't work,' when really they are
working 24 hours a day." (#136)

Injustice is also documented in the workplace. A report
from the diocese of Joliet found that the jobs predominantly held by women in the United States are in factory
service industries which employ women who are poor and
members of minorities. The data indicate that women are
most often concentrated at the lower and less lucrative
levels of all professions. (#139)

This and other studies also found that a higher proportion of women slip below the poverty line each year. A
significant number of these women are elderly, people
who fail to meet the glamorized stereotype of the ideal
woman and tend to be shunted aside when they have
outlived society's perception of their usefulness. A 1987
Census Bureau report indicated that elderly women have
a poverty rate 60 percent higher than that of elderly men.

They have small incomes, little savings and often live alone or in nursing homes. (#144)

The letter cites a specific comment from the Orlando diocese:

> Most of the poor are women. Women, especially those heading families, become poorer. In this quandary many turn to the church only to find:

> "The church so often seems cold and distant from the poor woman's reality. She often feels like a stranger and no one reaches out to her. She is embarrassed to share how she really feels and thinks. What will people say? It must not be right." (#146)

Not only do women face these pressures, the bishops find, but many suffer the double threat of sexism and racism. Less well educated than their male counterparts, most often charged with care of the children when residing in one parent families, and relegated to lower paying jobs, many women of color find it impossible to break the cycle of poverty into which they might have been born. Hispanic women report that their difficulties with the language barrier and with the Hispanic male's belief in the code of machismo add further blocks to their advancement in society.

Compounding all of this is the problem of violence against women in our society. "It is clear that violence against women is pervasive and extensive. Girls and women are victims of incest, rape, pornography, wife battering and sexual harassment." (#154)

The Bishops point out that the Church has called out for equal justice for women for over 100 years. They recommit themselves to continuing this public outcry supporting legislation on affirmative action that assures women equal opportunity and treatment and that does away with sex discrimination. (#169) Despite this, they recognize that the Church itself has had an uneven record in trying to satisfy such concerns within its own hierarchy. They call for greater education of male laity as well as priests, pastors, and bishops to "stress respect for the personal integrity of women and impress on males the sinfulness of violence and every form of sexual exploitation." (#173)

The bishops turn in their final chapter to the matter of "Partners in the Church." The Catholic Church, they point out, has always provided a place for women in its many enterprises including hospitals, schools, social services, and missions. But the bishops make a strong argument for increasing the potential for these women to occupy a greater share of leadership positions. Many women feel that they are ignored at the administrative levels of the Church, that their role has been to carry out decisions, not to make them. A participant from the diocese of Joliet noted:

> . . . the spiritual lives of women have been regulated and legislated almost exclusively by males, with clergy measuring women's virtue and spiritual growth against (the standards of) a male perspective. Often, too, double standards for men and women have been operative in the areas of morality as well as spirituality. (#186)

This disaffection is experienced by lay women and religious alike who observe that positions of power are most often given to men, even when more qualified women are available to fill these jobs.

The issue of equality for women within the hierarchy of the Church leads inevitably to the question of the ordination of women. Many valid arguments have been put forward in its favor, including the decreasing number of men now choosing to become priests. As one Kansas City participant cited by the bishops commented:

> Half the population is excluded from filling ur-
> gent needs in the church and society because of
> sex. Decline in priestly vocations has left a void
> in many areas of ministry. Yet, women are
> banned from meeting the needs of the people of
> God. (#198)

After identifying a number of ways in which women participate in the life of the Church, the bishops reiterate the official Church stand against the ordination of women as presented in the 1976 declaration *Inter Insigniores.* This document argued against ordination of women on the grounds that the Church has an unbroken tradition of refusing to ordain women and that this tradition, as a constant practice, reflects the mind of Christ by following his example. Despite this, the bishops call for further investigation and do not close the door entirely on the matter. The bishops advocate that all other offices not requiring ordination be opened to women.

In their conclusion, the bishops encourage women to maintain their involvement in the Church and continue to participate in a dialogue toward change. They end with a call for women to emulate Mary who stands "as a model for all Christians of what it means to be a partner with God in the work of salvation." (#239)

Reactions and Observations

The pastoral letter has stirred controversy since its first draft became public, including criticism from Rome. According to Susan Muto, a principal author of the draft, however: "Catholic women have been immensely ener-gized by the process." She also feels that the letter makes women's concerns universal concerns for the Church.[3]

Others believe that the Vatican's reaction, which has included a suggestion that the document be downgraded from a "pastoral letter" to a less authoritative "statement," is an attempt to diminish the significance of the bishops' efforts. As Archbishop William J. Levada of Portland, Oregon noted: "We run the risk of alienating women of deep faith and commitment if we find we have nothing to say to them."[4]

The idea that the Church might not have anything to say to women derives from the recognition that approval of the pastoral letter must be granted by Pope John Paul II, whose own published attitudes toward women have been criticized. Referring to the pope's 1991 encyclical *Centesimus Annus* on the hundredth anniversary of Leo XIII's *Rerum Novarum*, a national social justice organization of religious women took the view that John Paul II was continuing to treat women as "invisible" and was missing the reality of the conditions in which women find themselves today, especially in such matters as economic well being and family life.[5] Some matters, such as the pastoral's treatment of the ordination of women, deserve greater examination. Theologian Richard McBrien has outlined a number of arguments on both sides of the issue.

The arguments in favor of ordination include these:

1. The exclusion of women from priesthood violates human dignity and the baptismal mandate to participate in the mission of the Church according to one's qualifications, opportunities, and vocation.

2. Women have in fact served as deaconesses in the early Church.

3. There is nothing in Sacred Scripture which positively excludes the ordination of women.

4. Arguments against the ordination of women are deficient. For instance, Jesus called *no one* to ordained priesthood.

Opponents of women's ordination make these points:

1. The Church has maintained a constant tradition opposing the ordination of women.
2. Jesus called no women, not even his own mother, to priesthood.
3. The ordained priest represents Christ both spiritually and physically; this is known as "iconic representation."
4. No one has the *right* to ordination.
5. It is not clear that the early deaconesses were ordained.[6]

Because arguments exist for both sides of this issue, it may come down to necessity which ultimately changes the Church's position on women priests. The number of men wishing to take holy orders to join the priesthood has plummeted over the years. The Vatican maintains that this decline is a temporary aberration. But as fewer priests are available to minister to growing congregations, the question of women serving as priests might reach a point that philosophical ideals fall to hard realities.

The great accomplishment of the American Bishops' letter may reside in its creators' willingness to engage in controversial debates by raising questions about issues on which there is no absolute consensus. Presenting the voices of women openly discussing their concerns and their pain at what they feel are shortcomings of the Church is a positive step toward resolving these issues. Many people believe that the way the Church chooses to deal with these matters will have a profound effect on the institution as a whole for many years to come.

Endnotes

[1] National Conference of Catholic Bishops, *Partners in the Mystery of Redemption: A Pastoral Response to Women's Concerns for Church and Society* in *Origins,* Vol. 17, No. 45, April 21, 1988, #20. Further citations are by paragraph number.

[2] Paul Wilkes, "Profiles: The Education of an Archbishop," Part 1, *The New Yorker,* July 15, 1991, p. 58.

[3] Demetria Martinez, "Women and Rome: A Step Forward or Two Back?" *National Catholic Reporter,* June 21, 1991, p. 6.

[4] Peter Steinfels, "Policy on Women Hits Vatican Snags," *New York Times,* May 30, 1991, p. 5A.

[5] Amata Miller, IHM, "The Centennial Encyclical — Centesimus Annus," *Shaping a New World: The Catholic Social Justice Tradition 1891-1991,* Washington, D.C.: NETWORK, 1991.

[6] Richard P. McBrien, *Catholicism: Study Edition,* Minneapolis: Winston, 1981, pp. 852-853.

Christine Cherry Cernik

Unfinished Business: The Bishops' Pastoral on the Concerns of Women

A young medical student was once on the receiving end of constant criticism as she was assisting in the operating room. It seemed as if she could do nothing right. Finally, she began to prepare suture to stitch the patient's incision. Anticipating further reproach, she blurted out: "Shall I cut it too long or too short?" The six Catholic Bishops who prepared the 1988 draft pastoral on the concerns of women must have felt the same way.

The letter was criticized as "too liberal" by the Vatican and called "inadequate" by many of the Catholic women who had pushed for its creation. Bishop Joseph Imesch, who chaired the drafting committee, must have sensed that it would be controversial. How did he feel, he was asked, three years after the original draft came out? "Disappointed, I guess. Tired, but still hopeful."[1]

Entitled *Partners in the Mystery of Redemption: A Pastoral Response to Women's Concerns for Church and Society*, this document followed the bishops' two earlier pastoral letters on war and peace and on the economy. It grew out of the post-Vatican II era of heightened female consciousness.

Emerging Feminist Issues
The roots of "Catholic feminism" date back to the early years of the twentieth century. The Catholic Women's

Suffrage Society (also called St. Joan's Alliance) set out to acknowledge the compatibility of Catholicism and feminism in 1910. By 1959, with the announcement of the upcoming ecumenical council, the Alliance began to press for an expanded role for women in the Church, including even ordination as deacons.[2]

The Second Vatican Council (1962-1965) initially had no women delegates, a situation which prompted a protest from Cardinal Leon-Joseph Suenens that "half the Church was excluded from the Council's deliberations."[3] By the beginning of the second session 22 women auditors were appointed to two major commissions on the Church in the Modern World and on the Apostolate on the Laity.

Granted a voice, women were influential in assuring some mention of women's concerns, especially in the principal document *Gaudium et Spes* ("Joy and Hope") on the Church in the world. It noted that sex discrimination was "among the unjust prejudices that must be overcome and eradicated as contrary to God's intent."[4]

Pope John XXIII's 1963 encyclical *Pacem in Terris* emphasized that women, rejecting their portrayal as material objects, "demand rights befitting a human person in both domestic and in public life."

Neither the council nor the pope which summoned it addressed the issue of sexism within the structure of the Catholic Church itself. In the struggle to define a new role for women in the Church consistent with equality and dignity, traditional teaching had to be confronted. In truth, pre-conciliar Catholic doctrine, Pauline philosophy, and Scripture had rarely been interpreted to show equality between the sexes. But besides this theological problem, there were practical issues, both religious and secular, that concerned American Catholic women: birth control and women's ordination.

Pope Paul VI's *Humanae Vitae* (1968), rejected artificial contraception and provoked a storm of criticism. One commentator called it a "regressive moment in Catholic history."[5] Many Catholics found themselves unwilling to follow the pope's teaching.

At the same time in the religious sphere, Catholic nuns began to diversify their own ministries, responding to the call in the "Decree on the Renewal of Religious Life" (*Perfectae Caritatis*). They modified or even abandoned their distinctive religious dress to adapt to their new communities. Furthermore, many felt that they should work not only for charity but also for social justice. In addition, for some, admission to the ranks of the ordained ministry became a primary issue because they felt it a natural outgrowth of knowledge and spiritual development. Despite equal education, Holy Orders were reserved by tradition for men, and all laity and religious women were subordinate in this administrative structure. By the 1970's, a segment of vocal American nuns, in the Leadership Council for Religious Women formally aligned itself with the goals of the feminist movement.[6]

The Genesis of the Pastoral

The Church had acknowledged the human equality and dignity of women. Many women wanted these concepts extended within the institution itself, especially in regard to "inclusive language" (the removal of sex-specified text in the liturgy), openness to ordination, and a revision of hierarchical structure. In the International Women's Year of 1975, the Women's Ordination Conference (WOC) was organized and held its first meeting in Detroit. The primary goal, as its name implied, was to urge the ordination of women. The position of the hierarchy, voiced at the time by Archbishop (now Cardinal) Joseph Bernardin was simply that Tradition and Scripture had never accepted female ordination.[7] That is still the official position of the Church.

After two years of public protests by the WOC and other nonaligned women religious, staged at official events and ordinations, the National Conference of Catholic Bishops (NCCB) agreed to meet with the WOC to plan a dialogue and investigate the issue. The NCCB's Ad Hoc Committee on the Role of Women in Society had been established in 1972 to recommend action on women in the Church. In 1982, the committee recommended that the bishops address the issue through a pastoral letter.

By March of 1984, the drafting committee (six bishops and seven women consultants) was established and by November it decided to investigate.[8] The committee wanted to listen to Catholic women — those from national organizations and individuals on every level. In total, women from 24 associations, 60 colleges, and 45 military bases participated.

The listening sessions discussed broadly based questions asking women to define themselves in their roles as Catholic women, to enumerate their complaints and their spiritual needs found in the Church and society, and to speak of the themes they wanted the pastoral to address. The full questioning involved 75,000 Catholic women. The women and bishops on the drafting committee generally were not of extremist views, neither markedly conservative nor liberal.

Structure of the Pastoral

Amassing and organizing a vast group of concerns, letters, speeches, and feelings from 75,000 women presented a daunting task. To the uninitiated it might seem an odd way to proceed, for a social scientist or statistician might be looking for a more formal analysis of all the data presented. There was no attempt to rank, order, or statistically define significant issues. Instead, the bishops broke down the responses and concerns into four broad overlapping categories.

The first chapter ("Partners in Personhood") addresses women as persons and brings up the sentinel idea of the "sin of sexism." The second chapter ("Partners in Relationships") discusses sexuality and family structure, calling upon men to a higher, more active, responsible role within the family. It examines family planning and follows traditional Catholic teaching regarding contraception. The third chapter ("Partners in Society") urges the Church to provide equal pay for equal work and prepare priests for more compassionate counseling on sexual harassment and to be more sensitive to sexism. The last chapter ("Partners in the Church") opens the controversial issue of women's acceptance into the diaconate and all liturgical ministries that "do not require ordination."

Each chapter is divided into three parts. The women speak first, and are categorized into "affirming" and "alienated" voices. Quotations from women are used without specific citation other than the diocese they came from. Although most affirming voices commend the Church for its support of their roles as wives and mothers (the common theme), there is a "yes-but" quality to some of them:

> As I reflect upon my experience as a Catholic woman, what stands out the most for me is that I choose to participate in an institution that is discriminating against me as a woman. As a black woman, I would never even consider participating in any group that was blatantly racist — yet

I maintain membership in a church that is blatantly sexist. (#134)

The second part of each section assesses the "heritage" of prior Church teaching. The bishops bring to light the background of Church thought on issues of sexism, contraception, sexuality, and ordination. They quote biblical and encyclical sources, and present their comments in tempered fashion:

In regard to Christ's relationship with women:

Jesus' manner with women, as recorded in the Scriptures, was open, trusting, respectful and nothing short of revolutionary in a predominantly male-superior culture. (#205)

In regard to religious life:

In their renewal efforts, women religious have responded to the challenges facing all contemporary women. Their cooperation in the advancement of women in public and ecclesial life has in fact been encouraged by the church. (#214)

In regard to equal pay for equal work:

Women not only seek fair treatment in financial and legal matters; they want to uproot the basic causes of injustice in the anthropology, the psychology, the thought patterns and the presuppositions of our culture. Their cry for justice is not a passing complaint but a clear mandate for the church. (#162)

In regard to divorce:

The sacredness of marital fidelity is upheld by the sayings of Jesus opposing divorce and remarriage in the synoptic Gospels and stems from the perception of marriage as a permanent relationship between spouses. . . . Obviously, in a society where so many women are victims of abandonment and divorce, this teaching is countercultural. (#81, 82)

The third and clearly most controversial part of each chapter brings the bishops to the crossing of traditional Church teaching and reaction to the women's concerns. They must stand of two minds here: the first to hear the women, placing themselves empathetically with them; the second to examine themselves and their roles within a structured hierarchy that is being strongly criticized. Their goal was "to show thought and seek action" (#19), not to redefine women or prescribe roles. Reaction, criticism, and revision have primarily been focused on this section.

The topic which has attracted the most attention was a paragraph in the concluding part of Chapter One, which cited Minnesota Bishops Victor Balke and Raymond Lucker:

> . . . we are called to recognize that sexist attitudes have also colored church teaching and practice over the centuries and still in our day. Two of our brother bishops have done so already by defining the depth and heinous nature of this sin. "When anyone believes that men are inherently superior to women or that women are inherently superior to men, then he or she is guilty of sexism. Sexism is a moral and social evil." (#39)

Throughout the pastoral draft, the underlying issue is always sexism, whether it is defined in society, in partnership with men or husbands, or in Church hierarchy. Sexual exploitation, inequality, wife battering, violence in films, and the issue of women as equals in ecclesial roles are parts that make up the whole in examining sexism.

Bishop Imesch himself, however, urged that the pastoral not be read in pieces; focusing on this quote or that quote takes the draft further away from its original intent: to evaluate the much larger issue of the role of women in the Church, as well as to come to terms with the issues of family planning, sexuality, and single parenthood.

Reaction to the Pastoral Draft

The initial reactions to the draft encompassed lay and religious writers from academicians to the pope himself. It was noted in an editorial in *Commonweal* on the week of its publication that "the pastoral is not a work of critical analysis . . . not at the same level of theoretical sophistication as the pastorals on war and peace or the economy."[9]

Objections even focused on the pastoral's identification of the "sin of sexism." Phyllis Schlafly, well-known Catholic conservative, accused the bishops of "trying to create a new sin."[10] Conservatives objected to the "feminist excesses and the link between feminism and abortion."[11] Sister Mavi Coakley, a liberal critic, stated, "I was against them writing the letter in the first place and I haven't really changed my mind."[12]

Like Coakley, some liberal Catholic religious groups — such as the WOC — objected to the premise of the letter before it was undertaken as well as after it was written. Sister Mariella Frye, a member of the drafting committee, noted that women had cautioned the bishops "not to write a letter about women and what role they should be in and all that." She said, "Many women felt that a pastoral on women implied that women were the problem."[13]

Ruth McDonough Fitzpatrick of the WOC explained: "We reminded them that they did a letter on racism, not black people. They did a letter on the economy, not one on poor people. We told them to do a letter on sexism and the patriarchal hierarchical system."[14]

The methodology of the draft was frequently criticized as being too open to whoever shouted the loudest. There was concern that this represented a selection bias in data collection and also that these women had no formal bearing as experts. There was concern regarding the format of the analysis as well. Anne Patrick, vice-president of the Catholic Theological Society of America, remarked:

> It is not clear that moral theologians or ethicists have had such direct impact on the present draft [compared to the pastorals on war and peace and on the economy]. . . . It may be . . . that the limits set by Rome have ruled out from the start the most logical source of theologically trained analysis, for few if any Catholic women moral theologians are persuaded that official teachings on contraception and women's ordination can be justified in our day.[15]

Whatever its flaws in method, consensus opinion agreed that the problematic issues were those of defining the "sin of sexism" and thereby examining the concept of sexual equality, especially as it related to women's ordination.

Shortly after the pastoral was published, critic Monsignor John McCarthy lashed out against the "articulate feminist women who have rebelled against the teaching and have won the hearts of the writers." Using St. Paul (who urged wives to "be obedient to your husbands"), he argued that it is "divinely ordained" for men to hold ecclesial office and that in insisting on entry into orders, women are eschewing the "nature of womanhood." That there could be sexism in any fashion he rejected on the grounds of Pauline doctrine, and went on to state:

> For it is a faithful understanding of the Gospel of St. Paul that Eve sinned, not because she was a woman, but because she was a feminist woman, and Adam sinned, not because he was a man, but because he was a feminist sympathizer.[16]

Within several months of the draft and coincident with McCarthy's response, Pope John Paul II published a statement on "The Dignity of Women" (*Mulieris Dignitatem*). Styled as a "meditation," not an encyclical, it represented a personal reflection with some theological underpinnings. While not directly referring to the pastoral draft, it clearly came in response to the issue of sexism.

By quoting Paul's letter to Timothy — "For Adam was formed first, then Eve, and Adam was not deceived but the woman was deceived and became the transgressor" — John Paul put forth the traditional premise that the equality of men and women was broken by original sin. Because Woman was the initial transgressor, she "paid for" this by being subordinated to Man. Christ's death brought redemption for human beings from original sin and Mary became "the new beginning of the dignity and vocation of women." The pope dismissed the possibility of women's ordination by denying that Christ acted in a culturally conditioned manner in calling only men to be His apostles. He cautioned women to keep faith with the "Mary concept," not to expropriate male characteristics which are contrary to their own "feminine originality."[17]

Reactions to the document were mixed. Bishop Imesch took a positive approach. "It strengthens our own letter," he said.[18] Several feminist scholars argued that the pope avoided specific criteria for determining what in Scripture is definitive and what is mutable, a theme that has become a constant one in the theological arguments over "hermeneutics" (the interpretation of texts). If the pope would describe Scripture as mutable — a sharp and unlikely departure from traditional Catholic teaching — a broader theology might be open to an expanded role for women.

Mulieris Dignitatem did have a large impact on the rest of the body of bishops, as it was cited 20 times in the second pastoral draft completed in April 1990 and titled *One in Christ Jesus*. It seemed to placate those who felt the voices of feminism were too loud in the original document. Key points agreed upon in the two drafts were that both addressed Church discrimination against women and urged opening up all leadership positions not requiring ordination.

The second draft differed from the first by 1) deleting issues of birth control and ordination, 2) distinguishing Christian feminism from "radical feminism" and warning against "goddess worship" and pro-choice abortion philosophy, 3) endorsing inclusive language at a "human level," 4)calling for committees to develop plans from the dioceses and 5)emphasizing the "complementarity" of men and women rather than equality.[19]

In April of 1992, the bishops released the third draft of their proposed pastoral on the subject, entitled *Called To Be One in Christ Jesus: A Pastoral Response to the Concerns of Women for Church and Society.*

Reflecting reactions of the Vatican to earlier drafts, the document endorsed the Church's "unbroken tradition" of "calling only men to the ordained priesthood" and also gave more emphasis to Mary as a role model for women. The bishops continued their encouragement to the participation of women "in all liturgical ministries that do not require ordination" and added an injunction that a seminarian's "incapacity to treat women as equals" ought to be considered a "negative indicator for fitness for ordination." They maintained their condemnation of the "sin of sexism" and pledged themselves to work for equality of the sexes.[20]

Many voices are pressing for even further change. As prominent Church leader Sister Jolanda Tarango put it:

> The Pope and the bishops can define the role of women to their hearts' content. The issue is whether women today will live by the designs of the hierarchy. . . . Women are not sitting in expectation of the bishops' statements about who they ought to be.[21]

Endnotes

[1] "Bishop 'frustrated' by Vatican Consult on Women's Letter," *Florida Catholic*, June 5, 1991, p. 10.

[2] M. Francis Mannion, "The Church and the Voices of Feminism," *America*, October 5, 1991, p. 212. The term "feminism" refers to a multi-faceted movement dedicated to the understanding and attainment of appropriate roles of women in the Church and society.

[3] Rosemary Radford Ruether, "The Place of Women in the Church," in *Modern Catholicism*, Adrian Hastings, ed., New York: Oxford, 1990, p. 260.

[4] *Ibid.*, p. 261

[5] Robert G. Hoyt, "Sex: How Odd of God," *Commonweal*, July 15, 1988, p. 390.

[6] Ruether, p. 264. "Women religious" is a frequently used term referring to women who have taken vows and are members of a religious community.

[7] Joseph L. Bernardin, "The Ordination of Women," *Commonweal*, Jan. 16, 1976, p. 43.

[8] The drafters were Bishops Imesch, Matthew Clark, Thomas Grady, Alfred Hughes, William Levada, and Amedee Proulx, with consultants Mary Brabeck, Sister Sara Butler, Dr. Ronada Chervin, Dr. Toinette Eugene, and Dr. Pheme Perkins. Staff assistants were Sister Mariella Frye and Dr. Susan Muto.

[9] Editorial, "Dear John," *Commonweal*, April 22, 1988, p. 288.

[10] Abigail McCarthy, "Impossible, Twenty Years Ago," *Commonweal*, June 3, 1988, p. 327.

[11] *Ibid.*

[12] *Ibid.*

[13] *Partners in the Mystery of Redemption: A Pastoral Response to Women's Concerns for Church and Society,* in *Origins,* Vol. 17, No. 45, April 21, 1988, p. 761. Citations from the draft are given by paragraph number.

[14] Demetria Martinez, "Reactions to pastoral as varied as eyes of the beholders," *National Catholic Reporter,* June 21, 1991, p. 6.

[15] "Sexism, Sin and Grace," *Commonweal,* June 17, 1988, p. 366.

[16] John McCarthy, "The Bishop's Proposed Response to Concerns of Women," *Social Justice Review,* Vol. 79, No. 9-10, 1988, p. 147.

[17] "Excerpts from John Paul II's Apostolic Letter 'On the Dignity of Women,'" *New York Times,* September 30, 1988. The "Mary concept" is the traditional Catholic idea that the feminine role is based on an exaltation of the Virgin Mary — that she is the example for women as they should be in today's world.

[18] Peter Steinfels, "Anger and praise follow Pope's letter on women," *New York Times,* October 2, 1988, p. 8.

[19] "Second draft sidesteps controversial matters," *National Catholic Reporter,* June 21, 1991, p. 7. The concept of "complementarity" implies that it is appropriate that men and women have different roles in life.

[20] "Bishops issue third draft of women's pastoral," *Florida Catholic,* April 10, 1992.

[21] Martinez, p. 6. She is the national coordinator of Las Hermanas, an organization of Hispanic lay and religious women.

Lucy Fuchs

Grassroots Implementation of the Bishops' Pastorals

The American Catholic Bishops' three letters on peace and war, on the economy, and on women have been praised by some, criticized by others. Scholars have analyzed them; writers have commented on them; members of the clergy and religious have studied them. But the question remains: Have these letters reached the ordinary man and woman in the pew? Have they had any impact on the way people in the Church make decisions? In short, what has been the influence of these pastorals at the grassroots level?

Catholics and the Church

The Catholic Church is not a democracy; truth and authority are seen as coming from God down to the people. Doctrines in the Church are not developed by consensus, nor are Catholics traditionally asked to vote on Church laws or leaders. However, lay people have taken a much more participatory role in decision-making since the Second Vatican Council of the 1960s.

In the writing of the pastorals, the American Catholic Bishops have carried their consultation much farther than is usually done. Ironically, the bishops' attempt at widespread consultation and the writing of the pastoral letters on these topics of secular life, peace, economics, and women, have made some Catholics uneasy. They are the Catholics who have found the Church a so-called "comfortable pew." The Church provided services for them:

Mass and the sacraments, support in time of need especially illness and death, counseling when necessary, and celebration with them in joy. They did not expect the Church to challenge them, particularly not on public issues.

For many American Catholics, religion is "spiritualized" and morality "personalized." Someone who would never hurt a neighbor in any way could be involved in a war which harms non-combatants, or in tax fraud causing a loss of money for thousands, or in commercial decisions resulting in destruction of the environment. Religion is sometimes seen as a matter of private behavior, not public. For some, there is a clear line between the domains of God and Caesar.

When the Church issued these letters calling into question some aspects of Caesar's business, some Catholics became confused; others questioned the right and the competency of the bishops to speak on such topics. "The Church should not get involved in politics," was a common attitude.

But the more frequent response was simply to ignore the letters. The average American Catholic did not even read the summary version which accompanied each one. Diocesan newspapers reported on the pastorals; some parish priests gave homilies on them; workshops and conferences were held on them. But many Catholics reacted with indifference. Nonetheless, these pastoral letters have slowly seeped into the lives of American Catholics and have begun to change the Church.

The Challenge of Peace

The pastoral letter on peace was highly significant, not only because it took a stand on nuclear weapons, but also because the writing of this letter constituted the first time in the history of the American Church that the institution took advantage of extensive outside hearings and consultations, including U.S. policy-makers and military personnel, in addition to inside discussions with theologians. Three drafts were written by committees and more than 700 pages of responses of Catholics were evaluated. The pastoral represented an attempt to combine the truths of religion with a reading of the public issues of the day.

The letter was published in 1983 and was immediately hailed by some as forward-moving and by others as still too conservative. An editorial in *Commonweal* saw *The Challenge of Peace* as holding out the "potential of forging a new consensus in the nation's largest religious denomination."[1]

Theologian and writer John Garvey, on the other hand, wrote that the letter was weaker than the second draft had been which had called for an immediate end to the arms race. The letter, he said, "isn't prophetic, but it is a little better than no statement at all. A little."[2]

Then began the difficult work of promulgation.

One of the leading groups to welcome the letter was Pax Christi, a Catholic peace group. Although concerned that the bishops fell short of a full condemnation of nuclear weapons, Pax Christi immediately prepared materials for parishes to bring the issues of the pastoral home to the people.

The topic of peace was becoming an area of concern among Catholics. A study conducted by Notre Dame University in 1983 reported that Catholics were more supportive of a nuclear freeze than any other religious group. In fact, it found a startling 92 percent of Catholic parishioners in favor of a bilateral U. S.-Soviet halt on the production on nuclear weapons. The analysts interpreted this response as a direct result of the pastoral.[3]

Yet interest in the letter was complicated by concern with other life issues. Many bishops gave the topic of abortion a higher priority, thus leaving concerns for peace without a sense of moral urgency.

In this context, however, Cardinal Joseph Bernardin of Chicago and others articulated the "seamless garment ethic."[4] This approach takes the view that the moral case against nuclear war, abortion, capital punishment, and other social evils is one built on values that are inseparably linked. The seamless garment ethic is an attempt to build an internal consistency into the pro-life and anti-nuclear war issues. It holds that one who espouses any of these positions as indicative of the value of human life must needs embrace the others as well. Although this concept was well received in many quarters, large numbers of "pro-life" groups disagreed and held that each issue should be considered separately on its own merits.

In its assessment for 1985, Pax Christi expressed concern that the pastoral might be considered a "dead letter," as *Commonweal* writer Gordon Zahn also feared.[5] The Pax Christi statement insisted that if one judges by the criteria of the letter, the conditions for endorsing nuclear deterrence were not fulfilled. The organization urged the bishops to issue an additional statement, and reiterated its appeal in subsequent years.

By 1987 Pax Christi was expressing frustration:

> . . . we have found many reasons to be disappointed at what little has been accomplished since 1983 in the matter of disarmament. The military-industrial complex flourishes. There is little evidence that the general public, including the large Catholic population, is unhappy with a swollen defense budget, with repeatedly stalled

arms control talks, and with the continued development of new weapons systems.[6]

In 1990-1991 the peace movement was faced with the Persian Gulf War. It has been argued that all the meetings, protests, and movements toward peace did not stop this conflict which, in fact, had widespread popular support: 86 percent at the height of the war in February 1991.[7]

However, the pastoral letter, did have an impact. The National Conference of Catholic Bishops questioned the morality of the war. Although it fell short of condemning the conflict as a body, individual bishops spoke out against the war.[8] In addition, President George Bush found it necessary to try to make a public case that the conflict was a "just war."[9] Furthermore, there were scattered demonstrations across the country against the war, including one involving 150,000 on the Mall in Washington in January 1991.

When the war was over and the parades past, the euphoria on the part of many seemed to dissolve into an unsettling concern about the destruction of life in both Iraq and Kuwait, as well as a feeling that little had really changed because of the war. *Time* magazine even ran a cover story headlined: "Was It Worth It?"[10]

The fact that the question was being asked, and the heightened sensitivity about the so-called "collateral damage" of the war, are certainly in the spirit of the letter. Perhaps only the most sanguine of the bishops would have expected the thinking of American Catholics to change drastically with the publication of the pastoral, but at least such a change in thinking is a beginning.

Economic Justice For All

The economic pastoral was published after extensive consultation, including the input of the unemployed who had lost their jobs as a result of recession, or automation, or of the moving of a plant to an area of the world where labor is cheaper.

The letter was published in 1986 after three drafts. The bishops showed that they had learned from their experience. Whereas with the peace pastoral, they had only encouraged its reading and study, with the economic letter they established and funded a program for implementation. Created in 1987, a national office was responsible for translating the themes of the letter into education and action.

This office was especially concerned with collaboration within the Church and between Catholic organizations. In addition, individual dioceses set up their own programs. In the first eight months after the letter was issued, coordinators were in place in 130 dioceses. Buffalo, for example, established a full-time implementation officer almost immediately. In Atlanta, Father William Lyday made efforts to include lay persons in the newly established team. In Chicago and Louisville, leaders worked to bring the pastoral letter into the ongoing work of the catechetical ministries and the events of the diocese. In Youngstown, Ohio, Father Frank Lehnerd organized a diocesan study day to see how to apply the letter within the diocese. In Lafayette, Louisiana, coordinator Una Hargrove carried out a plan to train facilitators. In Scranton, Pennsylvania, Msgr. Constanti Siconolfi developed a broad-based task force which included trade unionists, attorneys, business people, state government officials, and university professors.

A west coast diocese established six implementation committees based on "action areas:" the preferential option for the poor, full employment, food and agriculture, the role of government, hospitals and social service, and Catholic schools. Another diocese put its money into a minority-owned bank with "just investment" policies. Others have coordinated with such organizations as the Poor People's Campaign, welfare reform coalitions, and self-help credit unions.

In 1987 alone the pastoral letter was discussed at conferences of more than 50 national Catholic organizations. The meeting of the National Catholic Education Association in New York City even included a visit with the poor.

This pastoral has been integrated into such Catholic organizations as the 3,000-member Christian Family Movement, the National Federation of Priests' Councils, and the Synod on the Laity. The Center of Concern's 1987 Summer Institute involved more than 200 people in studying the effects of proposed solutions to U.S. domestic social problems and their impact on so-called Third World countries, as well as on the international structural causes of poverty as reflected in workers' pay, interest rates, and land distribution around the world.

Some dioceses have begun working directly with the AFL-CIO in order to promote social justice. In September of 1987, the Connecticut state AFL-CIO passed a resolution entitled "Progress Toward a Just Social Order." It put the bishops' pastoral letter on the economy into perspective in terms of the waves of economic and social reforms that have prevailed over the past century.

In Rockville Centre, New York, a small committee of clergy and university and labor leaders helped organize the Long Island Labor/Religion Coalition to address, among other issues, the problems of the poor on Long

Island. This coalition now includes the diocesan Commission on Justice and Peace, the Long Island Board of Rabbis, the Unitarian Universalist Society, locals of the United Auto Workers, Electrical Workers' Union, American Federation of State, County, and Municipal Employees, and the International Ladies Garment Workers Union, as well as a number of non-profit housing organizations.

The pastoral letter has served as both the inspiration and justification for bishops to involve themselves in economic issues across the country. In Sioux Falls, South Dakota, and Sioux City, Iowa, for example, the bishops used the document in an attempt to mediate a labor issue that was having a severe impact on these communities. The dispute was between labor and a meat-packing firm with plants in both cities. Religious leaders worked with all involved.[11]

Other dioceses have gotten directly involved in political issues. Archbishop Charles Salatka of Oklahoma City and Bishop Eusebius Beltram of Tulsa issued a joint pastoral letter against passage of anti-union legislation proposed by the Oklahoma state legislature. They presented the Catholic social teaching that workers have a right to organize into unions. Sister Patricia Keefe, implementation coordinator for the pastoral, testified at the hearings. These efforts helped defeat the bill.

In Maryland, Catholics formed legislative networks to agitate for the passage of new programs to provide expanded pre-natal care and tax benefits for the poor. In Missouri, the Catholic Conference encouraged votes for assistance to family farmers. In the diocese of Green Bay, concern was focused on the passage of a jobs program. The dioceses of the state of Washington argued for an increase in the minimum wage. In Arlington and Richmond, Virginia, Catholic officials pushed for the passage of a bill on affordable housing.

Besides involving the Church in a myriad of projects correlated with local and national groups, the various dioceses began to ask themselves about the situation of their own people. Among the early responses to the letter were the actions that several of the bishops took to write their own pastorals on the economy, applying the principles to their own dioceses. Such letters and responses varied widely, depending on the circumstances of their people.

In Louisiana, a state which had experienced unemployment far above the national average, Bishop Stanley Ott issued a pastoral on the subject. Entitling the document "Hope: The Church Responds to Unemployment," he drew heavily on the national letter, applying it to the specific problems of Louisiana. He offered practical suggestions including committing specific funds to help in emergency situations and recruiting parishioners to work with the jobless, job-banks, day-care programs, and buyers' cooperatives.[12]

Among the other dioceses and states issuing their own letters was one from St. Petersburg, Florida, promulgated in 1988, and focused on such local problems as migrant workers, immigration, and a changing economy.

Many of the dioceses felt the need to set the pace and example for their lay members. *The North Carolina Catholic*, the newspaper of the Charlotte and Raleigh dioceses, published three issues on the national pastoral. A feature on "socially responsible investing" included for public discussion the stock portfolios of the two dioceses.[13]

In addition to examining their investments and other uses of Church money, Catholic leaders soon began discussing conditions for employees of the Church, as recommended in the letter. The National Association of Church Personnel Administration, a collaborative organization of clergy, religious, and lay Church leaders and ministers, published a document entitled "Just Treatment for Those Who Work for the Church."[14]

It is clear from these examples that the pastoral letter on the economy had an impact on the ordinary parishioner. Not only has it been studied, but programs have been developed throughout the United States. The impact of this letter has been greater than that of *The Challenge of Peace*. The reasons are two-fold: The bishops themselves made greater implementation efforts by establishing and funding an office of to put its ideas into practice; and since the economy touches the lives of all parishioners, there were many aspects in which lay persons could directly involve themselves and make changes at the local level.

The Concerns of Women

The proposed pastoral on the concerns of women was drafted by a six-member committee of the National Conference of Catholic Bishops, headed by Bishop Joseph L. Imesch of Joliet, Illinois. Seven women were designated official consultants, representing different academic disciplines and various cultural and vocational backgrounds. In the writing of the letter, extensive efforts were made to consult women themselves. Contacts were made with national organizations of women, and dioceses held "listening sessions." Other such sessions were held on 60 college campuses and 45 military bases. There were nearly 75,000 participants. The process constituted no doubt the largest opportunity ever extended to American Catholic women.

The first draft published, under the title *Partners in the Mystery of Redemption,* was actually the fifth draft written. It was significant in that it attempted to start from the grassroots level, looking at both the positive and negative experiences of women in the Church.

Following this draft, women were asked to read and respond to it at hearings held around the country. Response was spotty and in some places poor. Yet these sessions allowed women to meet in small groups and give their oral and written reactions to the proposed draft. However, it was clear that certain issues were not to be discussed, particularly the ordination of women to the priesthood.

The responses were returned to the bishops' committee, which then wrote a second draft in 1989 and a third in 1992. But the bishops did not promulgate it. The issue was becoming particularly controversial within the Church itself.

Rome pressed for global consultation on the subject. Vatican authorities suggested that the document not be issued as a "pastoral letter" but rather as a "statement," with less teaching authority. They also called for more emphasis in the document on Mary as a model for women, and on the themes of service and modesty. Furthermore, bishops from other countries took the position that this is a distinctly American concern and that women of other countries are not so alienated.[15]

Conclusion

Although few American Catholics have evidently read these three documents, their influence has not been minimal. On the contrary, the letters on peace and the economy have found their way into a change of attitudes on the part of not only American Catholics, but much of the public at large. The proposed pastoral on the concerns of women promises to be similarly influential. What is especially significant is the wide consultation and serious study the bishops have promoted on issues that concern the entire human family. Through their courageous efforts to listen to all sides and push forward in the face of criticism, the American bishops are changing the face of American Catholicism.

Endnotes

[1] *Commonweal*, May 6, 1983, p. 260.

[2] *Ibid.* p. 265. "Prophetic" in this sense refers to an inspired call from God to his people.

[3] Jim Castelli, "Do Catholics practice what the bishops preach?" *Salt*, Vol. 8, No. 5 (1988), pp. 20-21.

[4] Cardinal Joseph Bernardin, *Origins*, Vol. 13, pp. 491-94.

[5] Gordon Zahn, "On not writing a dead letter," *Commonweal*, March 8, 1985, pp. 141 ff.

[6] Pax Christi USA, *1986-87 Assessment Statement on the Challenge of Peace.*

[7] *Newsweek*, February 4, 1991, p. 25.

[8] Richard D. Parry, "The Gulf War and the Just War Doctrine," *America*, April 20, 1991, pp. 442-445.

[9] *Newsweek*, January 28, 1991, p. 64.

[10] *Time*, August 5, 1991.

[11] *Ibid.*

[12] *Working for Economic Justice*, Vol. 1 No. 1 (June, 1987).

[13] *Ibid.*

[14] *Ibid.*

[15] Joan Chittister, "Snowshoes in a mine field: U.S. bishops get nowhere," *National Catholic Reporter*, July 5, 1991, p. 18.

David T. Borton

Protestant Social Teachings

"What doth the Lord require of thee, but to do justly, and to love mercy, and to walk humbly with thy God?" (Micah 6:8) This biblical injunction reflects the spirit in which Protestant churches attempt to carry out their social mission.

Beginning with Martin Luther, John Calvin, and their followers during the Reformation of the sixteenth century, Protestant groups appeared in Europe, one after another. As they developed, they generally chose to determine doctrines and policies in community fashion, shaping their approach from below rather than through a hierarchy.

Especially in the twentieth century, Protestant churches have developed a varied set of social teachings. The process tends to follow these steps. First, a church convention might call for the study of an issue and commission a broadly based ad hoc group to examine the matter. The question is then taken up at a subsequent convention, debated, and decided. In this manner, the church examines issues ranging from the Christian response to the poor to the ordination of gays and lesbians.

The degree of authoritativeness of a teaching within Protestantism is not absolute. For example, theologian James Hudnut-Beumler summarizes the historical mood of his own church's assemblies: "No action of a church body can bind the conscience of any Presbyterian."[1] This observation of one denomination is representative of the general Protestant attitude toward authority. Within

Protestant social teaching, it is commonly understood that the individual Christian always bears the responsibility to choose what is correct in his or her life.

Three denominations illustrate varied positions in the social teachings of Protestant churches: the Presbyterian, the Episcopal, and the Methodist.

Presbyterians, Episcopalians, and Methodists

While there are 54.9 million Roman Catholics in the United States, Protestant groups are much smaller. The Presbyterian Church (USA) has 3.2 million members, the Episcopalian Church 2.8 million, and the United Methodist Church 9.5 million.[2]

The founder of Presbyterianism was John Calvin (1509-1564), a French reformer who had studied law and theology. While his intent may have been for reformation within the Catholic Church of his day, the Presbyterian Church was initiated by his followers after his death.

The Presbyterian Church (USA) is organized at the district level, with elected "superintendents." Ultimate power and authority, however, rests with the congregation. This church is the result of mergers of smaller bodies of Presbyterians which joined in 1983. Traditionally, the Scotch-Irish have been a dominant ethnic group in this denomination, but the situation is changing as Presbyterians intentionally seek a more heterogenous membership.

Presbyterians are among the most progressive advocates of social teaching. Among their "confessions," for example, is the Barmen Declaration, which originated in Europe in 1934 and endorsed resistance to the laws of civil government whenever they are in conflict with the "laws of the Kingdom."

The Episcopal Church bears the most similarity to the Catholic Church. Episcopalians have diocesan bishops and a presiding bishop who are elected to their positions. They are part of a world-wide communion called the Anglican Church or Church of England, which has as its symbolic leader the Archbishop of Canterbury. It traces its roots to the time of King Henry VIII (1491-1547).

Since the American colonial period, the Episcopal Church has traditionally been an influential body of societal influence and social power. (For example, while one percent of the American population is Episcopalian, 19 percent of the U.S. Senators are members of that denomination.) Its social teaching tends to be "middle-of-the-road," between Presbyterianism and Methodism. It is imparted through general convention statements and through bishops' pastoral letters.

The United Methodist Church traces its history to John Wesley (1703-1791), who was an Anglican priest in Great Britain. It has elected bishops but places more power at the congregational level than do Episcopalians. Methodists have a Social Creed, which underscores the social ramifications of the faith of each believer, as the faith is lived out in the context of culture. The Methodists incorporate the creed into their *Book of Discipline*, the central collection of church beliefs and procedures. In the U.S., Methodism grew most solidly among the middle class. It is well integrated, both racially and ethnically.

War and Peace Issues

All three denominations have formally dealt with questions of war and peace. They each generally accept the philosophy of "just" and "unjust" wars. They have also involved themselves in the controversies over U. S. military actions of recent years.

Presbyterians

Throughout the 1980s, Presbyterian assemblies debated such questions as U. S. military spending and arms sales, the validity of the 1983 action in Grenada and the so-called Contra War in Nicaragua, and moral aspects of nuclear war. These discussions led to a 1988 policy statement called "Christian Obedience in a Nuclear Age." It took the position that, since obedience to the state has limits, each individual must apply his or her conscience case by case on each specific issue of war and peace. Through the application of Just War theory, the document went on to condemn nuclear war and the assembly called for the elimination of nuclear arms.[3]

Like many Protestant groups, Presbyterians have established their own independent peace organization. The church also supports the concept of "civil disobedience:" that is, the open and non-violent breaking of laws in order to demonstrate their injustice, and with a willingness to pay the penalty. Moreover, Presbyterians take the view that peace cannot prevail unless justice is present.[4]

Episcopalians

The Episcopal Church in recent years has taken up a number of war and peace issues at its annual conventions.

In 1982, for example, the church took what could be considered a middle-of-the road position on the use of force, justifying it on a case-by-case basis depending on the context of the legitimacy of the end. The convention's summary document encouraged "the mutual reporting of successful ways of including in dialogue persons with differing viewpoints." It went on to commend the church on its work in behalf of the poor and encouraged the production of educational materials to put the war and peace issue before its members.[5]

The 1988 general convention, while accepting the possession of nuclear armaments, created a permanent office on peace and justice and endorsed the work of the Anglican Peace and Justice Network.[6]

Methodists

This denomination rejects coercion, violence, and war as incompatible with the Gospel. As a group, Methodists oppose compulsory military service and challenge what they consider the militarization of American society.[7]

To that end, the church encourages governments to abolish "tools of war." In 1972, the Methodist Bishops rejected the U.S. nuclear arms deterrent policy. The church links justice with peace, proposing that more support be given to the United Nations, specifically the International Court of Justice. It recommends that the U.N. serve an expanded role in achieving human rights, that agencies within the U.N. not be dominated by the developed world, and the U.N. assist in achieving new levels of economic justice throughout the world.[8]

The Historic Peace Churches

Churches which have long been noted for their pacifist principles include the Mennonites (along with their early derivatives, the Amish and the Hutterites), the Church of the Brethren, and the American Friends (commonly called the Quakers). They total 394,000 members throughout the United States.[9] They have a distinctly resolute stance on peace.

Each of these churches was formed in Europe during the 16th-18th centuries. They are the only Protestant groups which have built into their tenets that under no circumstances is a person of faith to resort to violence, either in daily life or through service as a member of the military.

The activities of one group, the Mennonites, illustrate the kinds of things these churches are doing to carry out their principles. This denomination has an Illinois office called the Lombard Mennonite Peace Center, which teaches mediation and methods of non-violent conflict resolution. It also serves as a professional mediation service to industry and to the church at large. The Mennonite Central Committee was founded in 1920 to respond to natural disasters like floods and earthquakes. Today, it has professionals deployed throughout the world to provide agricultural, technical, medical, and nutritional assistance. It is highly respected within the international community.

The Church and Economics

Protestant social teaching was strongly influenced by Martin Luther and John Calvin. Both elevated work (a calling or vocation) for the everyday person to a level of importance on a par with the calling to the priesthood. Over the years within Protestantism, there has been an understanding that work is a "trust from God." Furthermore, the accumulation of capital is seen as good as a means of production and as an investment tool which is to bear interest. As such, Protestantism has fostered the growth of the free market, capitalistic system.

Only in the twentieth century has the Protestant Church of the U.S. attempted to reexamine its historical relationship with the free market system. Protestant social teaching has shifted in this century from a strong advocacy of capitalism to a position which questions economic forces and structures which may have become inherent obstacles to economic justice for all. The church now seeks out systemic causes of what it considers "oppression" within all economic systems.

Presbyterians

Since the 1970s, the Presbyterians have taken a distinctly progressive social within the Protestant Church. They have called for a review of the denomination's investment policy and were among the first to endorse economic boycotts, for example, against corporations doing business in apartheid South Africa, and against the Nestle company for "profiteering" by marketing infant formula in parts of the world where mothers could least afford it.

The church has also paid particular attention to those without food, shelter, or medical care. As James Hudnut-Beumler puts it: "In Presbyterian social teaching on economic life, there is a presumption in favor of equal sharing of economic benefits and burdens, and there is a clear test of how well any system or policy is working; namely, how does it treat the poor?"[10]

Recent Presbyterian general assemblies have called for decent housing as a basic human right, along with full employment and a guaranteed annual income. They have also endorsed welfare reform, work incentives with education and training components, and adequate child care for low income workers.

In the view of the Presbyterian Church, there is a direct relationship between heavy military spending and corresponding increases in the number of people living at the poverty level. The church has called not only for decreased military expenditures, but also for a reduction in the national debt (to ease the inflation burden on the poor) and changes in the tax structure for more progressive rates.

The Presbyterians have not been shy about addressing so-called "North/South Hemisphere" issues: lowering trade barriers to developing nations; stabilizing world commodity prices at just levels; transferring resources from the rich to the poor nations; and searching for economic models which discourage urban growth and at the same time, emphasize traditional and communal values.[11]

Episcopalians

The Episcopalian Church has a long record of progressive positions on economic issues. In the early years of the twentieth century, the church called for a just and fair return to the worker, equitable distribution of wealth, and the elimination of poverty.[12] In this period, it was particularly influenced by socialists within the Anglican community, most notably William Temple (1881-1944), the leading archbishop of in Great Britain in the 1940s.

In more recent years, the church has initiated what it calls the "Jubilee Ministry concept" to carry out its social teaching. Ventures have included inner-city housing projects, day-care, and programs for street people, with emphasis on doing ministry with the poor.

In 1982, the urban bishops of the Episcopal Church issued a Labor Day Pastoral. While it is unofficial, it sounded with a ring which some progressive critics generally find missing from the official speech of the church. The bishops reiterated labor's right to organize and called for economic models other than the prevailing free market system, which they felt puts sole emphasis on the maximization of profits. They also urged the church to stand with communities reeling from corporate dislocation and endorsed the democratic ownership of corporate resources.[13]

Some critics feel that, despite these actions, the church has been too slow on these issues. Episcopalian theologian Robert Hood notes: "The economic teachings of the Episcopalian Church . . . have been weakest in their failure to examine critically some of the basic tenets of the market ethics at work in the U.S. economy and corporate culture."[14]

Methodists

The Methodist Church presents the majority of its positions on economic social teaching in its *Book of Discipline.* The church holds that all economic systems are under the judgment of God.

It speaks out in favor of full employment, minimal inflation, adequate incomes, the reduction of the concentration of wealth in the hands of a few, revision of the tax structure, and the elimination of government support programs which benefit only the wealthy. The church also calls for the creation of new ways to share resources more equitably: food, clothing, shelter, education, and health care.

Furthermore, the Methodist Church has taken positions in support of adequate income maintenance, job training, meaningful employment, and the humanization of welfare programs. It counsels against lotteries as a regressive tax on the poor. It calls for limitation on private property for the greater needs of the community on the argument that government should respect the rights of the whole society, not just the individual. It has condemned the selfish spirit of the market system, endorsed a collaborative approach to collective work agreements, and stressed human needs before profits.[15]

Protestants and Women's Issues

Presbyterians, Episcopalians, and Methodists ordain women to the ministry. Along with some Lutheran groups, they employ biblical criticism and see Scripture as containing time-bound language and outdated social customs. As such, prohibitions to women clergy have fallen within many Protestant groups.

All three denominations permit abortion, under church guidance. They have also attempted to promote sensitivity to women's concerns in general.

Presbyterians

Presbyterians have had ordained women clergy since 1962. There remain, however, questions of equity as to staff church assignments, relationships within multiple staff, and to salary differences among women and men. By 1979, the Presbyterian General Assembly mandated representation by women on all boards and commissions. Assemblies also endorsed passage of the proposed Equal Rights Amendment to the U.S. Constitution and have repeatedly highlighted the issue of domestic violence against women. The 1984 assembly raised particular concern about the "feminization" of poverty and recommended more federal funds for children's health programs, child care, and education.[16]

Moreover, the Presbyterian Church has been working with the National Council of Churches on Scriptural language inclusive of both men and women, in place of the traditional masculine references.

Episcopalians

The Episcopal Church first approved women for ordination in 1976, although unauthorized ordinations occurred earlier during the 1970s. (One of the participants in the unauthorized ordinations, Barbara Harris, is now an Episcopalian bishop in Massachusetts.) The presiding bishop of the Anglican Church of New Zealand is a woman. Women's ordination, however, is not universal throughout the Anglican community.

Archbishop George Carey, head of the world-wide Anglican community (appointed by the Queen of England), made headlines shortly after his installation when he endorsed this still-controversial practice. "The idea that only a male can represent Christ at the altar is a most serious heresy," he said. Although he later tempered his remarks to term it a "fundamental and theological error" rather than "heresy," it was a strong statement on the place of women in the church.[17]

The inclusion of women within the decision-making process is far from complete. While the new president of the Episcopal House of Deputies, Pamela Chinnis, celebrated her election in 1991, she was quick to point out that only 22 percent of the leadership positions within the Episcopalian Church are held by women.[18]

Methodists

This denomination has a well established record of women clergy. Some of the predecessor bodies of the United Methodist Church licensed women to preach as early as 1866. Full ordination rights for women were sanctioned in 1956.

Over the years, women's issues have been a recurring theme at conventions. Resolutions have included a review of committee membership for inclusiveness, training for ministers to assist women in crisis, and support within the Methodist Church for the International Women's Decade, 1975-1985.

Summary Observations

Catholic Archbishop Oscar Romero of El Salvador once wrote: "We are a pilgrim church."[19] This sentiment applies to the social teachings of Protestant churches, as well. These are not "end" positions. Discussions and resolutions surface again and again.

Within Protestantism, the believer bears the responsibility for a decision. Each must weigh the church's teachings or statement on a particular issue and ultimately make the decision his or her own.

The content of Protestant social thought may at times seem superficial. For example, the 1991 Episcopal General Convention dealt with 600 resolutions. Such "resolution theology" can make a convention feel good about itself as it returns home, but little legacy is left to the church in the way of substantive theological reflection and resultant social teaching.

Protestant denominations which see themselves in relationship with the greater church invariably have more progressive social teaching than do isolated denominations. As a general observation, the more a denomination limits its definition of salvation to an exclusively spiritual term, the less the denomination calls forth to its members on matters of justice. There is some disappointment among Protestants that many of the more theologically conservative denominations have no declaration for justice within their social teaching.

Finally, the members who attend conventions and set these social teachings tend to come from the progressive elements of their denominations. When the resultant social thought is reviewed by Protestants in the pew, it is not universally accepted.

It is this pilgrim church which must continue to find its way "to do justly, and to love mercy, and to walk humbly" with God.

Endnotes

[1] James D. Hudnut-Beumler, "The Rights and Dignity of Persons," *Conscience and Justice* Vol. 81, No. 2 (November 1990), p. 20.

[2] *The Florida Catholic*, August 2, 1991, p. 20. Frank S. Mead, *Handbook of Denominations in the United States*, Nashville: Abingdon Press, 1985, p. 107-225.

[3] Hudnut-Beumler, pp. 112-113.

[4] *Ibid.*, p. 103.

[5] The Joint Commission of Peace, *To Make Peace*, Cincinnati: Forward Move Publications, 1988, pp. 20, 21.

[6] *Ibid.*, pp. 31-37.

[7] Ronald P. Patterson, ed., *The Book of Resolution*, Nashville: Abingdon Press, pp. 103-104.

[8] *Ibid.*, pp. 435-437.

[9] Mead, pp. 63-153.

[10] Hudnut-Beumler, p. 76.

[11] *Ibid.*, p. 80-81, 83. The lowering of trade barriers comes with mixed blessings. If a poor nation turns its productive capacity away from the basic needs of its people, export may cause additional poverty.

[12] *Journal of the General Convention*, quoted in Robert E. Hood, *Social Teachings in the Episcopal Church*, Harrisburg, Pennsylvania: Morehouse, 1990, p. 58.

[13] Hood, p. 172.

[14] Ibid., p. 177.

[15] Ronald P. Patterson, ed., *The Book of Discipline — The United Methodist Church*, Nashville: Abingdon Press, pp. 96-98.

[16] Hudnut-Beumler, pp. 40-42.

[17] *The Episcopal Life*, April, 1991, p. 8.

[18] *Journal of the General Convention, 1988*, quoted in Hood.

[19] Oscar Romero, *The Violence of Love*, trans. and ed. by John R. Brockman, San Francisco: Harper & Row, 1988, p. 3.

Kathleen Kosuda

The Social Teachings of Judaism

In an ancient compilation of rabbinical teachings, there appears the following story which illustrates the very essence of Judaism:

> It happened that a certain heathen came before Shammai and said to him, "Convert me on condition that you teach me the entire Torah while I am standing on one foot." Shammai drove him away with the builder's measuring stick that was in his hand. He then came before Hillel who converted him. Hillel said to him, "That which is hateful to you, do not do to your neighbor. This is the entire Torah; the rest is commentary — go and learn it."[1]

Some consider this the source of the Golden Rule. It is often told to affirm the importance of ethical behavior as an example of doing to others what one would wish done to oneself. Certainly, it is indicative of Judaism's tradition of regard for others, which is the fundamental principle of the religion of Judaism.

According to ancient teaching, the commandment, "Thou shalt become a blessing," was given to Abraham by God. It is considered by some commentators the maxim with the most meaning in either Jewish or universal human ethics. The commandment implies one is not alone, that actions and aspirations fulfill their purpose through the lives of others.[2] Ideals of proper behavior were held to apply not only to the Jewish population but to the whole of humankind.[3]

The Nature of Judaism

What is Judaism? In its essence, the word has two meanings. It refers to the civilization of the Jewish people, and it also means the spiritual aspect of that civilization, its religion. Jewish theology affirms one God and is the source of the Christian religion, not only in its monotheistic doctrine but also in its traditions of martydorm, proselytism, monasticism, and liturgy.[4]

Judaism centered on books, especially the Torah (the Hebrew word for "law" or "doctrine").[5] The Torah is the first portion of the Jewish Bible, the Old Testament of Christianity, consisting of the Five Books of Moses or Pentateuch: Genesis, Exodus, Leviticus, Numbers, and Deuteronomy. The second section of the Bible is called Prophets, the third Writings.[6] To most Jews the Torah is both law and tradition; to fundamentalists (such as Orthodox Jews) it is the revealed Word of God.[7]

The Talmud, written by ancient rabbis and second in importance to the Torah, is made up of two distinct books, The Mishnah and the Gemarah. The Mishnah is the recorded Oral Law of the Jews and dates from the year 200.[8] Essentially, the Mishnah is commentary on an elaboration of the Torah, and the Gemarah is a commentary on the Mishnah.[9]

The Torah and the Talmud are monuments to tradition. All aspects of Jewish life, from worship to paying wages, from mathematics to medicine, are regulated by these and other important texts.[10] Historically in some areas, one book may have been more important, after the Torah, than another. The books of the Prophets, extensions of the Torah, are explicated by the Writings. Other books are the

Midrash, Siddur, and Zorah. Also, the works of the philosopher Maimonides were treasured by some groups. The beliefs and practices of Judaism have been documented in books for more than three thousand years.

Development of the Jewish Tradition

Judaism has not had a unilateral history; it has developed with various segments. It has also sprouted a tradition of social responsibility and charity. Judaism has differing world views, a historic pattern of central and then decentralized authority, and even populations dissimilar in customs and practices relating to their geographical regions. The "ism" of Judaism suggests a system of law, philosophy, and ethics, but the Jewish population is a distinguishable people and a nation, not just a voluntary group of believers.[11]

There have been two tendencies in the Judaic world view, especially in the religious sector, one toward insularism and the other toward a more universal perspective. These views have opposed each other throughout history, in some circumstances one prevailing over the other. The insular or particularistic advocate sees all rules and principles in the Judaic tradition as being of equal importance. Futhermore, contact with non-Jews has even been forbidden in some instances. Acceptance of all religious regulations without distinction and rejection of outside influence are essential in the Judaism of this constricted vision.[12]

The universal view, on the other hand, sees the essence of Judaism as the promotion of human development, and gives priority to these principles over the other religious regulations. As M. Lazarus explained: "Completely expressed, it is the ideal at once of the Jew and of the whole of mankind, and the highest promise and tenderest hope held out by Judaism is that all nations may unite in the common effort to approach its realization."[13] Consequently, contact between the Jewish people and all others is encouraged. The conflict between these two world views has continued into the present.[14]

Judaism has developed from a narrow authoritarian tradition to one with a more diffused focus. Until the eleventh century there was a central religious authority to which the Jewish population deferred, and until the nineteenth century, each Jewish community was tightly organized. However, there was always a degree of latitude, and today each congregation is autonomous, free to choose its rabbis and determine its own polices.[15]

During the course of history, Jews have been distinguished as Ashkenazic or Sephardic, each with different practices and customs. This distinction was also geographical: Ashkenazic Jews lived in Germany (in Hebrew *Ashkenaz*) and Europe; Sephardic Jews lived in Spain (*Sepharad* in Hebrew), and spread throughout northern Africa and the Middle East. Today, approximately three-fourths of all Jews are Ashkenazic.[16]

In America, there are three major branches of Judaism. Orthodox Jews are the most traditional in matters of theology, practice, and liturgy. The Torah is held to be divinely revealed and a religious observance is woven into daily life. The dietary laws (a set of regulations originating in the Bible governing food consumption) are strictly obeyed. The Conservative branch sees religion as evolving from a scholarly, historical approach to Judaism, and traditional practices such as the dietary stipulations are less strictly regarded. The reform branch is the most liberal, adapting Jewish thought and practice to a modern outlook. Rituals are fewer and food restrictions are peripheral to the religious observance.[17]

Charity

The idea of charity in the Jewish religion is connected to ethical behavior. This appears in the Bible, for example, as caring for the poor (Deuteronomy 15:17-11) and defense of the widow and orphan (Exodus 22:21-23). The prophet Amos (5:15) said, "Hate evil and love good and establish justice in the gate;" his words are frequently quoted as an edict of how to behave.

However, responsibility for the welfare of others is not merely a commandment of Judaism. It is regarded as law. One of the passages which goes to the heart of tradition is in Deuteronomy (15:7-11):

> If, however, there is a needy person among you, one of your kinsmen in any of your settlements in the land that the LORD your God is giving you, do not harden your heart and shut your hand against your needy kinsman. Rather, you must open your hand and lend him sufficient for whatever he needs. Beware lest you harbor the base thought, "The seventh year, the year of remission, is approaching," so that you are mean to your needy kinsman and give him nothing. He will cry out to the LORD against you, and you will incur guilt. Give to him readily and have no regrets when you do so, for in return the LORD your God will bless you in all your efforts and in all your undertakings. For there will never cease to be needy ones in your land, which is why I command you: open your hand to the poor and needy kinsman in your land.

Thus, the mandate may be interpreted to give to the poor and to give gladly, especially in light of another fundamental commandment: ". . . you shall love your neighbor as yourself." (Leviticus 19:18)

In 1201, the philosopher Moses Maimonides codified the Talmudic rules in the Eight Degrees of Charity or the Laws of Giving to the Poor, each one higher than the one following:

1. The highest degree, exceeded by none, is giving a gift or a loan or taking one as a partner or finding him employment by which he can be self-supporting.
2. Giving charity to the poor without knowing to whom one gives, the recipient not knowing the donor's identity, for this is a good deed of intrinsic value, done for its own sake. . . .
3. Giving to one whose identity one knows, although the recipient does not know the donor's identity. . . .
4. Giving without knowing to whom one gives, although the recipient knows the donor's identity. . . .
5. Giving before being asked.
6. Giving only after being asked.
7. Giving inadequately, though graciously.
8. Giving grudgingly.[18]

Maimonides also said, "If the poor asks of you and you have nothing to give him, soothe him with words." Maimonides urged hard work and suffering rather than being dependent on others. Even a learned person who is poor should work at a trade rather than ask the community for money, he said.[19]

An early characteristic of Judaic giving was the rightness of choosing to give; having choices and obligations was part of the covenant with God. The concepts of right and good, always associated with the care of the individual and society, were basic to Jewish values and ethics for centuries even beyond the spectrum of a formal religion. It was thought that God lived through human actions and that obedience to God and His teachings in doing right would yield everlasting peace and well-being.

The emphasis of Judaism is in *this* world, not in the afterworld. Life must follow God's teaching because what cannot be accomplished during life cannot be accomplished after life. While there is belief in the "world to come" where the soul will exist forever, the purpose of life is to perfect the soul by acting properly. The concept of charity for the purpose of salvation was never part of early Judaism; charity simply was a basic religious obligation.

Jewish faith in God was also expressed through being part of a community. Freedom to choose humanitarian actions assured a good society, not just for Jews but for all people. This is considered God's goal — a perfect society. To be disobedient, to thwart one's relationship with God, is a sin and, since disobedience also impinges negatively on the community, God's purpose is denied. A person's relationship is not just with God but with fellow beings. To follow God's teachings is to be right and good and to be compassionate to others.

There is no word for "charity" in Hebrew. The word used in that sense is tzedakah which literally means "righteousness." It has been defined as "the fulfillment of an obligation to a fellow being with equal status before God. It is an act of justice to which the recipient is entitled by right, by virtue of being human."[20]

Another word for charity is *mitzvah,* meaning "a divine commandment."[21] In the modern vernacular, a *mitzvah* could be described as an assertive charity: not just giving to the poor who happen to come to the door, but going out and seeking them. Additionally, the importance of maintaining the dignity of the person receiving charity is of concern, and so tradition has emphasized anonymous assistance. For centuries synagogues have had charity boxes with the sign *Matan Beseter* (Hebrew for "fitting gift"), indicating an anonymous donation.[22]

Furthermore, since human beings are created in God's image, to do justice to others is to do justice to God. Injustice is desecration. Jewish tradition even states that "the poor man does more for the rich man than the rich man for the poor man."[23] Refusal to give charity is considered to be idolatry.[24] To this day, Jewish funeral practices call for modest burials because the grave makes everyone equal.[25]

The influence of Judaism on early Christian charity was direct. Many ideas in the New Testament regarding Christian giving (Matthew 25:35-36) have Hebrew antecedents. The concept of reward in the afterlife for giving charity or of punishment for not providing charity, however, developed only in Christianity.

Through the centuries the Jewish community formulated a complex system of public welfare. In the second century the allocation of funds was still simple. All members of the community were taxed, even recipients of charity, and two basic funds were then provided, one of money and one of food. By the Middle Ages market prices were regulated so that the poor could purchase food and rent at cost. [26] Later on, benevolent societies were formed for different purposes, like visiting the sick and providing clothing. One such association — The Bread, Meat, and Coal Society — dates back to 1779.[27]

Large national and international philanthropic groups, like the United Jewish Appeal and Hadassah, now channel social services funds to those in need.

According to the advice of the Jewish sages, society is never absolved of its responsibility for the welfare of others. No one is beyond human concern or beyond repentance and rehabilitation. A person may fall four or five times but others must continue to offer strength. [28]

The Jewish Religion and Economic Justice

There is no pronouncement on economic justice from Judaism similar to the Catholic documents *Rerum Novarum* or *Economic Justice for All*. Several reasons have been advanced. Charles Strain says that the Jewish religion is based on law with ethics an intrinsic aspect. Christianity, on the other hand, he says, is faith-based, deriving ethics from theology.[29]

Another reason offered is that Judaic law is not highly systematized. Rather it is a collection of teachings which traditionally are searched by scholars for interpretations on various issues, including economics. The Judaic economic order has been addressed, therefore, through laws and practices derived from the Bible, the Talmud, and other religious literature.[30]

The closest parallels to Catholic pronouncements are various statements by the Union of American Hebrew Congregations, the American Jewish Congress, the American Jewish Committee, and the National Jewish Community Relations Advisory Council. While representing diverse groups, they all call for a social agenda which meets human needs. The statements do not all speak from a theological point of view, and they are not set forth in a large context or with systematic analysis.[31]

Historically, Jewish society had an authoritative religious tradition in their literature for every facet of life, including the economy. However, secularization in the last few centuries has seen the weakening of ideological and institutional mechanics of traditional Jewish life.

Jewish ethics is now pluralistic, and pronouncements on behalf of all Judaism are difficult.[32]

War and Peace in Judaism

There are many references to war throughout the Bible, some of which condemn war and violence (Genesis 49:57, I Chronicles 28:2-3) and others which advocate it. In the twelfth century, Maimonides wrote, "He who fights with all his heart, without fear, with the sole intention of sanctifying the Name, is assured that no harm will befall him and no evil overtake him." He indicates that war will bring peace: ". . . there will be neither hunger nor war, neither jealousy nor competition."[33]

The ability to begin a new life after a period of suffering is central to the message of the Hebrew prophets, and it is the main component of the covenant between God and Abraham.

In contemporary times, those who work for peace see the partnership in the covenant as a demand to work for peace and justice as well as to dialogue with Israel's neighbors. Some see Israel as becoming an isolationist state   contrary to the spirit of Judaism, if peace in the Middle East is not found.[34]

Acknowledging that the mixing of religion and politics is a constant in religious history, whether the political entity is a Biblical tribe or a modern nation-state, does not placate those concerned about current events. The establishment of modern Israel in 1948 was both a secular and a religious accomplishment, and Israel's Independence Day is celebrated in different ways. For example, non-observant Jews celebrate with family and friends, perhaps going on an outing. Religious Jews recite special prayers of thanksgiving to God; for them, establishment of Israel was more a religious than a political act.[35] Few Jews deny their right to maintain a sovereign state, but those yearning for peace may decry the similarity of modern conflicts in the Middle East to battles fought by Biblical ancestors.

The ideal of the Jewish religion is not just peace, but peace and truth and justice (Zechariah 8:16,19). Peace alone can mean oppression and suppression; without peace, truth and justice are ineffective. In the classic Jewish texts, these are almost always mentioned together, because they are regarded as inseparable and interdependent.[36]

Women in Judaism

The women's movement of the last few decades has been a source of religious renewal for Jewish women.[37] Traditionally, they could not be religious leaders or participate in communal worship, but by the mid-1980's almost 50 percent of the students entering the more progressive rabbinic colleges were women.[38] In 1984, the Conservative Jewish Theological Seminary began admitting women to rabbinic training.[39]

There is, however, an ongoing debate concerning the treatment accorded women in the historic Jewish community. The community was considerably in advance of other societies, even though it demeaned women according to one view.[40] Others believe that Jewish practice elevated women to a place of special honor and, indeed, certain historic women were given high status in early Judaism. Sarah, wife of Abraham and mother of Isaac, and Ruth, the Old Testament heroine who refused to desert her mother-in-law, are women whose names and deeds were not lost to history.

Nevertheless, the Bible dictated subservience for the average woman. "You shall be eager for your husband, and he shall be your master." (Genesis 3:16) This and similar passages have led to a very low status for women in general through most of Jewish history.[41]

As Jewish women continue to participate more fully in their religion, there may be a reversal of the impact which religion had on women's lives. Instead, women may have a significant influence on religion, especially women on Judaism, since it lacks the strong authoritarian hierarchy of Catholicism and the bureaucracies of mainline Protestant religions.

Summary

Jewish teachings are based on the Bible and other books which document beliefs and practices. The basic principle is concern for others. The Bible is also a source of the ideals of truth, justice, equality, goodness, and peace, all of which are central to the values and beliefs of the Jewish social tradition. Established in the tenets of the Bible, these traditions have been interpreted for centuries in the rabbinical and philosophical writings of the great Jewish thinkers. Judaism is an ethical system as well as a formal religion concerned with human behavior. Its fundamental principle of the Golden Rule is a guideline of timeless value.

Endnotes

[1] *Babylonian Talmud,* quoted in Barry W. Holtz, *Back to the Sources, Reading the Classic Jewish Texts,* New York: Summit, 1984, p.11. Hillel (c.70 BCE-c.10 CE) was a prominent Jewish teacher, known for his wisdom and founder of a school, Bet Hillel. Shammai (c.50 BCE-c.30 CE), also a teacher in the first century, founded a rival school, Bet Shammai, and was similarly celebrated for his religious zeal.

[2] Wilhelm Jerusalem in Ismar Elbogen, "Fundamental Views of Morality," in Simon Bernfeld, compiler, *The Foundations of Jewish Ethics,* Armin Hajman Koller, translator, New York: KTAV, 1968, pp. 61-62.

[3] M. Lazarus, *The Ethics of Judaism,* Part I Henrietta Szold, translator, Philadelphia: Jewish Publication Society, 1900, p. 189.

[4] *The New Encyclopedia Britannica, Macropaedia,* volume 10, Fifteenth edition. Chicago: William Benson, Inc. 1975, p. 315.

[5] Milton Steinberg, *Basic Judaism*, New York: Harcourt, Brace, 1947, pp. 19-21. The word Torah can also be used to refer to the entire Bible and to all religious books of the Jews. Steinberg, pp. 21-23, discusses an even broader meaning, that of "tradition."

[6] The Jewish Bible differs from the Catholic Bible in the order and number of books and in excluding the twelve books of the Apocrypha, and from the Protestant Bible in the order and number of books.

[7] Harry Gersh, *The Sacred Books of the Jews*, New York: Stein and Day, 1968, p.16.

[8] There are two Gemarahs, the Palestinian and the Babylonian, each a record of comments and discussions of the Mishnah by different schools of rabbis, sages, and scholars.

[9] Gersh, pp. 104, 122.

[10] *Ibid.* pp. 12-13.

[11] Jonathan Webber, "Between Law and Custom & Women's Experience in Judaism" in Pat Holden, editor, Women's Religious Experiences, London: Croom Helm, 1983, p. 144.

[12] Lazarus, pp. 213-214.

[13] *Ibid.* p. 214.

[14] *Ibid.* p. 215

[15] Geoffrey Wigoder, *The Encyclopedia of Judaism*, New York:Maclillan, 1989, pp. 176, 534, 591.

[16] Shmuel Himelstein, *The Jewish Primer*, New York: Facts on File, 1990, p.23.

[17] Steinberg, pp. 152-153.

[18] Arthur Hertzburg, *Judaism*, New York:Braziller:, 1972, pp. 106-107.

[19] *Ibid.*

[20] Richard G. Hirsch, "There Shall Be No Poor," in Milton R. Konvitz, editor, *Judaism and Human Rights*, New York: Norton, 1972, p. 239. Barry W. Holtz, *Back to the Sources: Reading the Classic Jewish Texts*, pp. 20-21, notes that "Tzedakah is often defined as charity but this misses the point of the Hebrew word's origin which means justice and righteousness. Charity comes from the latin "caritas" meaning love or caring, an act dependent on the good will of the giver, not on the obligation to act for the sake of justice.

[21] *Ibid*, p. 240.

[22] *Ibid.* pp. 240-241.

[23] Ruth Rabba 5:9, 19 in Hirsch, p. 239.

[24] Tosephta Pe'ah 4:19 in Hirsch, p. 239.

[25] Hirsch, p. 241.

[26] *Ibid.* pp. 244-245.

[27] *Encyclopedia Judaica*, Jerusalem: Keter, pp. 376-377.

[28] Hirsch, pp. 243-244.

[29] Charles R. Strain, editor, *Prophetic Visions and Economic Realities*, Grand Rapids: Eerdmans, 1989, p. 77.

[30] *Ibid*, pp. 77-78.

[31] David Biale, "Jewish Statements on Social Justice" in Robert McAfee Brown and Sydney Thomson Brown, *A Cry for Justice: The Churches and Synagogues Speak*, New York: Paulist, 1989, pp. 70-72.

[32] Strain, pp. 77-78.

[33] Joel L. Kraemer, "On Maimonides' Messianic Posture" in Isadore Twersky, editor, *Studies in Medieval Jewish History and Literature*, Cambridge: Harvard, 1984, pp. 132-136.

[34] Haim Gordon, "Beyond Fatalism: Education for Peace within Judaism" in Haim Gordon and Leonard Grob, editors, *Education for Peace; Testimonies from World Religions*, Maryknoll, N.Y.: Orbis, 1987, pp. 58-59.

[35] Himelstein, p. 230.

[36] Milton R. Konvitz, editor, *Judaism and Human Rights*, New York: Norton, 1972, p. 277.

[37] Charles E. Silberman, *A Certain People*, New York: Summit Books, 1985, pp. 262-263.

[38] *Ibid.*

[39] *Ibid.*

[40] Julia Neuberger, "Women in Judaism: The Fact and the Fiction," Pat Holden, editor, in *Women's Religious Experience*, London: Croom Helm, 1983, p. 132.

[41] *Ibid.*, pp. 136-137.

John J. McTague

The Social Teachings of Islam

Islam is a religion about which there are many misconceptions. The general perception in the United States is that Islam is anti-western and belongs to an alien culture with which the West has little in common. However, nothing could be further from the truth. Islam has strong ties to both Judaism and Christianity and regards itself as following in their traditions. Some of the similarities are as follows:

First, all three are monotheistic religions which reject any type of idolatry. Yahweh, God, and Allah are essentially different names for the same Deity. Second, all three religions trace their origins to the Old Testament prophet Abraham. Muslim tradition teaches that Abraham travelled to Mecca and built the Ka'aba there to house the Black Stone he was given by the angel Gabriel.[1] Moreover, one of the two major holy days in the Muslim calendar is the Id al-Adha, which commemorates Abraham's willingness to sacrifice his son in order to please God.

Islam accepts Judaism and Christianity as its antecedents and recognizes the Old Testament prophets and even Christ, although only as a prophet and not as God. Muhammed, the founder of Islam, never claimed to be divine but only described himself as the last and greatest of the prophets. Islam also preaches belief in heaven and hell, a judgment day, existence of angels and devils, and moral conduct as the path to eternal salvation. The religion also has a sacred book, the Quran (commonly rendered "Koran"), which contains the word of Allah as revealed to Muhammed.

General Beliefs and Practices

Islam is often described as not just a religion but a complete way of life.[2] It provides detailed instructions for human behavior in all aspects of life and warns believers that it is by their deeds that they will be judged by Allah. Allah's guidelines for humanity (*sharia*) form the basis of Islamic law, for which Muslims acknowledge four sources. First is the Quran, which Allah presented to Muhammed gradually from 610 A.D., when the Prophet first began his mission, until his death in 632. The Quran, roughly four-fifths the length of the New Testament, is a litany of advice arranged into chapters (*suras*) which traditionally appear according to length, the longer ones first. Since it is the word of God, it must be adhered to, although much of it is open to interpretation.

The second source for Islamic law is the Sunna of the Prophet, which includes things he said, did, and permitted others to do while he was alive. Since Allah said in the Quran "if you should quarrel over anything refer it to God and the Messenger" (Q 4:59).[3] Muslims believe that the Sunna (the behavior of Muhammed) is an authoritative source of law. It has been preserved in reports known as hadith, some of which have had their authenticity challenged.

A third source is the use of reason in interpreting both the Quran and the Sunna, for as time went on issues arose for which neither source provided clear-cut answers. Consequently, a class of legal scholars (*ulama*) and judges (*qadis*) arose to decide proper behavior in new situations, based on their knowledge of Islamic traditions:

When faced with new situations or problems, scholars sought a similar situation in the Quran and Sunna. The key is the discovery of the effective cause or reason behind a Sharia rule. If a similar reason could be identified in a new situation or case, then the Sharia judgment was extended to resolve the case.[4]

The fourth source, consensus of the community, is an extension of the third. If over the course of time a majority of *ulama* and *qadis* accepted one particular interpretation of the Quran or the Sunna, that view became the recognized one.

From these four sources a highly extensive and detailed legal code has developed over the centuries to encompass every aspect of life. The best known and most important laws are the duties known as the Five Pillars of Islam.

The Pillars of Islam

All duties and obligations are divided into those owed to Allah and ones directed toward the community. The Five Pillars are duties of the first type, which is what gives them such enormous significance. They are as follows:

1. The profession of faith (*shahada*): a Muslim must proclaim, "There is no god but Allah and Muhammed is His Prophet." This statement affirms the believer's commitment to monotheism and acceptance of Muhammed's special role in the development of Islam.

2. Prayer five times per day (*salat*): seven days a week Muslims are expected to recite brief prayers at the following times: daybreak, noon, mid-afternoon, sunset, and evening. These prayers can be said wherever the person happens to be at the time, at home, at work, or at play. On Friday, Islam's holy day of the week, the noon prayer

should be performed in a mosque at a group service led by a prayer leader (*imam*).

3. Almsgiving for the poor (*zakat*): all adult Muslims who can afford to do so are obliged to pay an annual tax of 2.5 percent of their wealth and assets to help the less fortunate in the community. The Quran specifically states:

> Alms shall be used only for the advancement of Allah's cause, for the ransom of captives and debtors, and for distribution among the poor, the destitute, the wayfarers, those that are employed in collecting alms, and those that are converted to the faith. (Q 9:60)

4. Fasting (*siyam*) during Ramadan: the month of Ramadan, the ninth in the Islamic calendar, is a time when all healthy adult Muslims must abstain from any food, drink, or sexual activity from sunrise to sunset each day. Consequently, they must rise before dawn to eat their first meal and wait until sundown for their next. Since the Islamic is a lunar calendar and is eleven days shorter than the solar one, Ramadan rotates through all four seasons, creating special hardship during the longer, hotter summer days.

5. The pilgrimage to Mecca (*hajj*): every Muslim who is financially able to do so is expected to make the pilgrimage at least once in his or her lifetime. This should take place during the twelfth and final month of the Islamic year, Dhu al-Hijja, and it involves a number of prescribed rituals carried out over a ten-day period.

Themes

Community is a constant theme in Islam. One of the most famous passages from the Quran reads: "You are the noblest community that has ever been raised up for mankind. You enjoin justice and forbid evil." (Q 3:110)

The religion stresses the group far more than the in-dividual, much as Christianity did during the Middle Ages. Individual human dignity is seldom mentioned, although each person is held accountable for his or her behavior before Allah.

The duties toward the community, while not given as much emphasis as the Five Pillars, regulate each Muslim's behavior toward his fellow human beings and are ex-tremely detailed. Some of the better known rules are the bans on alcohol, pork products, and gambling for all practicing Muslims, and the allowance of up to four wives at a time for men. Also under the heading of obligations toward the community are attitudes toward economics, women, and warfare.

Another theme is the equality of all believers. Despite any differences in rank or wealth, all people are equal in the sight of Allah, and they will be judged strictly on their piety and behavior.

And finally, there is a strong streak of social justice running through Islam. Numerous passages in the Quran condemn exploitation of debtors, women, orphans, slaves and the poor; others are critical of unethical business practices and ostentatious wealth.

Sects Within Islam

Much like Christianity and Judaism, despite an essential unity of belief, disputes have arisen within the Islamic community which have led to the emergence of different sects.[5] The major division is between the Sunnis (from Sunna, the sayings and actions of Muhammed), who com-prise roughly 85 percent of the world's Muslims, and Shi'ites ("partisans" or "party"), who make up the other 15 percent. This split developed quite early in Islamic history, originating only thirty years after the death of

Muhammed (632 A.D.) After the Prophet's passing, leadership was handed down to men who were his closest companions. Each of these men in turn was designated "caliph," successor to Muhammed as leader of the community. The fourth caliph, Ali, was the Prophet's son-in-law, having married his daughter Fatima. Ali had assumed his position in 656 after the assassination of his predecessor and his failure to find the murderers prompted two revolts against him. Ali himself was murdered in 661 during the second of these rebellions, and the caliphate passed to the Umayyad family, relatives of the previous caliph.

But the supporters, or partisans, of Ali refused to acknowledge defeat and rallied around his second son, Hussein. In 680 he rose in rebellion against the Umayyads but was defeated and killed in the battle of Karbala. This incident gave the Shi'ites a second martyr and created their world view of themselves as an unjustly persecuted minority who are the true followers of Islam. They elevated Ali and Hussein to a status almost equal to that of Muhammed, and their burial sites at Najaf and Karbala respectively (both in modern-day Iraq) became the major Shi'ite shrines. Shi'ites refused to recognize the authority of the caliphs and insisted that only descendants of Ali were legitimate rulers (*imams*).

The origins of Sunni Islam were characterized by expansion, conquest, and success. By 732 its empire included the entire Middle East, North Africa, Central Asia and Spain. But those of Shia Islam were forged in defeat and martyrdom.

Today, Shi'ites make up the overwhelming majority of the population of Iran, are the largest religious group in Iraq, and form significant minorities in Lebanon and the Persian Gulf sheikdoms. Otherwise, in the Middle East,

North Africa, and other Muslim countries such as Pakistan, Bangladesh and Indonesia, Sunnis predominate. The two groups have generally coexisted peacefully, but the Ayatullah Khomeini succeeded in reviving the Shi'ite sense of persecution in the 1980s, which has caused renewed tension between the two sects.

The Shi'ites themselves are divided into three major groups and among the Sunnis there are four schools of law, each of which is dominant in some part of the Muslim world. The result has been a lack of central authority to make definitive decisions with regard to religious doctrine. There is no equivalent in Islam to the Pope, a leader whose pronouncements are regarded as authoritative. The position of caliph, created after Muhammed died, combined religious and political leadership but the caliphs were never considered experts in theology or law. But even the caliphate has been abolished, by Mustapha Kemal Ataturk of Turkey in 1924, leaving Islam with no unifying figure whatsoever. Consequently, the views of the Islamic faith on topics relating to social issues are not derived from some *ex cathedra* pronouncement but rather from a combination of the four sources: the Quran, the Sunna, reasonable interpretation, and consensus of the community. Most scholars attempt to justify their views via reference to the Quran.

A further problem, common to most religions, is the gap between theory and practice. The expressed teachings of Islam are often ignored. One finds contradictions between doctrines and common practice in the Muslim world. Nevertheless, the focus here is the beliefs of Islam, not the behavior of individual Muslims.

Economics

Scholars of Islamic economics in recent years have regularly made comparisons with capitalism and socialism, but their conclusions are far from unanimous.[6] Consider these contrasting opinions:

> Indeed, it may be argued that the main difference from capitalist systems will be the absence of interest as a source of income and that the main difference from a socialist or centrally planned economy will be Islam's acceptance of private property rights.[7]

> One of the first points emphasized by author after author is that Islamic economics is not capitalism minus interest plus zakat or socialism minus state control plus Allah. It is something unique and different and exclusive to Islam.[8]

Despite this disagreement, most discussions of Islamic economics center around five issues: almsgiving, interest, property rights, profit, and economic equality.

Almsgiving (*zakat*) is the most familiar of these issues, since it is one of the Five Pillars. As such it is a specific obligation for every Muslim, which can not be ignored. (Q 22:79) Islamic governments assumed the duty of collecting it, a practice which continues today in some states, notably Saudi Arabia, where it substitutes for income tax. The normal rate is 2.5 percent annually, collected on all assets, not just income. The state also assumes the responsibility of seeing that the money is disbursed in a proper manner.

The second issue concerns charging interest on loans (*riba*). The Quran condemns usury (excessive interest) in no uncertain terms (Q 2:275-8) but over time Islamic scholars have extended the prohibition to include all fixed interest. This ruling, of course, has caused great difficulty for those in the banking business and in modern history most banks in the Muslim world have simply ignored it. Their chief defense has been the argument that since the Quran specifically condemns usury, reasonable rates of interest are acceptable in the eyes of Allah.

But the Islamic revival of the past two decades has looked askance at that interpretation, and as a result institutions known as "Islamic banks" have been established in a number of Muslim countries. These banks neither give nor charge fixed interest rates. Instead, they pay and receive "dividends" based on the profit or loss of a particular investment. In other words, if the bank makes money in a given year, its depositors share in the profits. Similarly, when the bank loans money, it earns a portion of the profit of that project (or the loss). While such banks might sound impractical to a westerner, for a growing number of people in the Third World who wish to live by the tenets of Islam, they are a godsend.

With regard to property, there is no question that the Quran recognizes the right to private ownership, for there are numerous references to it throughout the holy book. However, this right has a considerable number of restrictions attached to it. First is the fact that "to Allah belongs the kingdom of the heavens and the earth. He has power over all things." (Q 3:190) All property acquired by humans is held in trust for Him. (Q 35:40) Also, property must be acquired via strictly legal and ethical means; bribery and deception are forbidden. (Q 2:189)

Once property and wealth have been accumulated, the owner's behavior is closely regulated. Ostentatious wealth is condemned (Q 4:38) but so is miserliness and hoarding of money. (Q 3:181; 9:34) The rich are frequently exhorted to share their bounty with those less fortunate. (Q 30:39; 23:64; 17:27; 74:7) This advice extends beyond mere almsgiving, which is a requirement.

Similarly, business and commercial activity are frequently commended (Q 2:198; 2:275; 4:29) but with numerous caveats. Muhammed himself was a merchant, running the caravan trade of the widow Khadija, who eventually became his first wife. Basically, Muslims are enjoined to follow fair business practices: contracts should be negotiated fairly and set in writing (Q 2:283); full measure should be given in all transactions (Q 83: 1-7); goods that are sold should be of high quality. (Q 4:3)

According to one scholar, Ayatullah Mahmud Taliqani of Iran:

> . . . the simple law of supply and demand in the usual capitalist understanding cannot direct transactions. This is because demand in the usual capitalist usage and in actuality depends on the ability to buy things and on having money. But demand, on the basis of Islamic jurisprudence, arises out of what is actually required by necessity. Therefore supply and the actual making available of goods will be limited to what is actually required by necessity. The marketplace thus cannot become the toy of the greed of capitalists by which they open the way to false demand and oppressive profit.[9]

Discussion of the issues of property and business activity leads inexorably to the topic of economic equality and inequality. Islam preaches that all people are equal before Allah but this does not mean that they must be equal in material possessions. The Quran states "to some of you Allah has given more than to others" (Q 16:72) and "do not covet the favors by which Allah has exalted some of you above others." (Q 4:32) As one scholar put it:

Islam then, does not demand a literal equality of wealth, because the distribution of wealth depends on men's endowments, which are not uniform. Hence absolute justice demands that men's rewards be similarly different, and that some have more than others — so long as human justice is upheld by the provision of equal opportunity for all.[10]

The inequities are also tempered by all the strictures of the religion: the requirement to give alms; the ban on interest; and the restrictions placed on property ownership and business. Thus, while Islam does not demand economic equality in the communistic sense, those inequalities that do exist are supposed to be limited to the extent that no one lives in poverty while others are in luxury.

Other aspects of economics mentioned in the Quran are inheritance and gambling. The holy book gives specific and detailed instructions on how property and wealth are to be divided among relatives, some of which will be discussed in the next section. (Q 4:7-12) As for gambling, the directive could not be more straightforward: "Believers, wine and games of chance, idols and divining arrows, are abominations devised by Satan. Avoid them, so that you may prosper." (Q 5:91)

When all these directives are looked at together, one finds an economic code not much different from the Jewish and Christian traditions. Individuals are encouraged to make a profit and acquire property but to do so through ethical means and to avoid excess. Inequalities of wealth are permitted but the rich must never forget the less fortunate. One major difference is almsgiving, which is encouraged in the other two religions but mandated in Islam. The other unique feature is the prohibition on interest, but even this concept was accepted by the Christian Church prior to the Reformation. All three faiths emphasize that economics must serve the good of the community as a whole, not just the individual.

Women

While few people in the U.S. are familiar with Islamic views on economic issues, most have heard "horror stories" about the religion's attitudes toward women.[11] The status of women in Muslim countries has been as significant as any other factor in contributing to the image of Islam as a backward, anti-western belief. Several of the most controversial aspects of women's concerns are marriage, divorce, inheritance, and the veil.

The subject of marriage in Islam is a source of endless condemnation in western countries. The Quran states that "you may marry other women who seem good to you; two, three or four of them." (Q 4:3) This phrase has been interpreted to mean that a man can have up to four wives at any one time; women, however, are allowed only one husband. This seeming injustice has been defended as an improvement over pre-Islamic times in Arabia, when men were allowed an unlimited number of wives, and as keeping women from a life of spinsterhood in a society which had a shortage of men. Moreover, the Quran follows the above statement with the warning, "but if you fear that you cannot maintain equality among them, marry only one" (Q 4:4) and later in the same *sura*, "try as you may, you cannot treat all your wives impartially. Do not set yourself against any of them." (Q 4:129) Thus, polygamy was considered the exception rather than the norm and one scholar estimates that today it is practiced by less than 10% of the world's Muslims.[12]

Islam also gave males the privilege of marrying outside the faith while denying it to women. (Q 5:5) On the other hand, women were allowed to keep their dowries (Q 4:4), which were part of the marriage contract. Marriage in Islam is just that, a contract rather than a sacrament. It has been explained this way by one scholar:

> The relationship of a husband and wife is viewed as complementary, reflecting their different characteristics, capacities, and dispositions, and the roles of men and women in the traditional patriarchal family. The primary area for men is the public sphere; they are to support and protect the family and to deal with the "outside" world, the world beyond the family. Women's primary role is that of wife and mother, managing the household, raising children, supervising their religious and moral training. While both are equally responsible before God to lead virtuous lives, in family matters and in society women are subordinate to men by virtue of their more sheltered lives, protected status, and the broader responsibilities of men in family affairs. (Q 4:34)[13]

Another cause of misunderstanding in the West is divorce in Islamic countries. The common perception is that a Muslim man can divorce his wife simply by reciting three times: "I divorce you." However, this practice contradicts the words of the Quran, which explicitly tell all believers to wait three months before finalizing a divorce. (Q 65:1-5) Unfortunately, the "instant divorce" has been legalized in most Muslim states but it is considered to be sinful for a man to take advantage of it.

Women can also initiate divorce proceedings in Islam, but not as easily as men. In that regard the Quran said that "women shall with justice have rights similar to those exercised against them, although men have a status above women." (Q 2:228) Unlike men, women seeking a divorce must have specific grounds. These grounds include non-support, abuse, desertion, impotence, and insanity. But Islamic courts generally award children of a broken marriage to the father, which along with women's difficulty in earning a living in the Muslim world, has tended to dissuade them from seeking divorces.

Actually, Islam considers divorce a last resort. The Quran suggests arbitration between quarrelling spouses (Q 4:35) while a popular *hadith* claims that "of all things permitted, divorce is the most abominable with God."[14]

Another issue is women's right to property. The Quran establishes a precedent in specifically allowing wives to keep their dowries. Women are also given a right of inheritance, although only half of what men receive. (Q 4:11) The holy book says: "Women shall have a share in what their parents and kinsmen leave; whether it be little or much, they are legally entitled to their share." (Q 4:7) This again was a change from pre-Islamic Arabia, where women had no inheritance rights whatsoever.

Still another source of western scorn is the custom of women veiling themselves in public. The origin of this practice is the Quranic injunction to "enjoin believing women to turn their eyes away from temptation and to preserve their chastity; to cover their adornments (except such as are normally displayed); to draw their veils over their bosoms and not to reveal their finery except to their husbands, their fathers [and other male relatives]." (Q 24:31)

Whether this passage mandates complete coverage of women in public can be debated, but the fourth source of law, consensus of the community, eventually accepted that interpretation. It is noteworthy, however, that since the Iranian Revolution of the 1970s and 1980s, veiling has become more common among women throughout the Muslim world. A recent article noted that "the veil may be a symbol of oppression to the Western eye, but to many who wear it, it is freedom — not just from the tyranny of Western culture but also from unwanted sexual advance."[15]

Overall, westerners need to understand that Muslims do not view women's issues the same way they do. As analyst Jane Smith explains:

> It is crucial to see that for the Muslim the message of the Quran is eternal, divine, and absolutely, authoritative. If the Quran says that men have authority over women, it is important to understand that the context is one of care and responsibility, but even more important to respect the statement as God's final word. Therefore, to talk about equality in Western terms is to be out of tune with the Muslim understanding. The issue is not equality per se, but complementarity. A commonly stated interpretation is that God has created men and women with different constitutions and differing roles, and the task of each husband and wife is to work toward the kind of true cooperation that God intends.[16]

Warfare

As with the topic of women, warfare in Islam has been a subject of much controversy in the West.[17] Evening news videos of both Ayatullah Khomeini and Saddam Hussein declaring holy war (*jihad*) against the United States conjure up images of Muslim fanatics fighting to the death to defeat the infidel. Here again the gap between perception and reality is a large one. Even the word *jihad* is often misinterpreted. Technically, it means "striving" or "exerting oneself" to support Islam, and the sword is only one of four means by which that can be accomplished. The others are by the heart, the tongue, and the hands.

The Quran speaks against the evils of war, warning that "whenever they kindle a fire for war, Allah puts it out. They strive to create disorder in the earth, and Allah loves not those who create disorder." (Q 5:65) On the other hand it also says: "Have faith in Allah and His apostle and fight for His cause with your wealth and your persons," promising eternal reward for those who do so. (Q 61:10-13; 4:74) It was this injunction that inspired the followers of Muhammed to sweep out of Arabia in the century after his death to conquer an empire extending from Spain across North Africa through the Middle East up to the borders of India. They divided the world into the *dar al-Islam*, which they ruled, and the *dar al-Harb*, which they did not yet control.

> The dar al-Islam was in theory neither at peace nor necessarily in permanent hostility with the dar al-Harb, but in a condition which might be described as a "state of war", to use a modern terminology, because the ultimate objective of Islam was to establish peace and justice with communities which acknowledged the Islamic public order. But the dar al-Harb, though viewed as in a state of nature, was not treated as a no-man's land without regard to justice. Islam proposed to regulate its relationship with the dar al-Harb in accordance with a branch of its law called the Siyar.[18]

Siyar became the Islamic equivalent of international law: rules governing relations with the non-Islamic world. While found neither in the Quran nor the Sunna, these rules developed from decisions of scholars based on situations that existed once the tide of Muslim conquest waned after the Battle of Tours in 732. Certain Quranic verses were used to justify a less militant attitude toward the outside world: "There shall be no compulsion in religion." (Q 2:256) "Fight for the sake of Allah those who fight against you, but do not attack them first. Allah does not love the aggressors." (Q 2:190) "If they incline to peace, make peace with them, and put your trust in Allah." (Q 8:61)

In other words, when the Islamic world was powerful and expansionist in its early years, *jihad* was interpreted as aggressive war to extend the territory under Muslim control. But the inability of Islam to subdue the rest of the world, evident by the ninth century, and the breakup of the Muslim empire into rival states, which began at the same time, meant that aggressive war would be perpetual war. Consequently,

> in those altered circumstances, scholars began to change their position on the question of whether the jihad, used against unbelievers on the grounds of their hostility to Islam, was just. The doctrine of the jihad as a duty permanently imposed upon the community to fight the unbelievers wherever they might be found retained little of its substance. . . . No longer construed as a war against the dar al-Harb on the grounds of disbelief, the doctrine of the jihad as a religious duty became binding on believers only in the defense of Islam.[19]

This concept of *jihad* as strictly defensive war has remained the dominant interpretation since at least 1000 A.D. All other types of warfare except *jihad* are forbidden, based on the Quran's condemnation quoted above (Q 5:65), so Muslim leaders in modern times have always declared their wars to be *jihads* in order to gain the support of the public. But these ploys have seldom gone unchallenged. In World War I the Ottoman Empire declared holy war against the Allies but Sharif Hussein, the governor of Mecca, rebelled against the Turks (Lawrence of Arabia's famous campaign). In the past decade, most Muslim governments ignored Khomeini's call for *jihad* against Iraq (a fellow Islamic state) and Saddam's patently false holy war vs. the U.S. Probably the last widely accepted *jihad* was the defense of the Holy Land against the Crusaders in the Middle Ages. Today, with the absence of a single recognized leader of Islam, it is unclear who could authentically call for a *jihad.*

Even in a legitimate war, there are strict rules of conduct for Muslims. All treaties must be respected, even those with non-Islamic states. (Q 8:73) Muslims must fight fairly unless the enemy first breaks the rules, but if he lays down his arms then the Muslim must do so also. (Q 2:190-3; 8:62-3) Any of the enemy who surrender or are taken prisoner must be treated humanely. (Q 47:4-5)

Overall, it appears that Islamic views on warfare are in harmony with those of Christianity and Judaism, now that *jihad* is regarded as defensive warfare exclusively. *Jihad* can be considered the Islamic equivalent to the Christian concept of "just war," although they do not match precisely. Of course, if Muslim nations often ignore these tenets, so do Christian ones.

Conclusion

In two major areas — economics and warfare — Islam is in reasonably close touch with Judeo-Christian traditions and current doctrines. The one area where there appears to be a gap is on the status of women. But here it might be useful to remember that the "liberation" of women in the West has taken place quite recently, mostly in the last thirty years. Islam is in roughly the same position as the Catholic Church before the Second Vatican Council (1962-1965), which liberalized many Church doctrines. The difficulty for Islam is that, in the absence of any centralized authority, it would be extremely difficult to accomplish something similar over a short span of time. As a result, Muslims are likely to remain at odds with the West on the status of women in society for the foreseeable future.

The main doctrines of Islam were formulated during its dynamic and creative era, which ended before 1000 A.D. These ideas have changed very little since then. While many observers in the West see the religion as hopelessly outdated, the strong Islamic revival of the 1970's and 1980's seems to refute that notion. Each religion must answer one question: Are its doctrines eternal or must they change with the times? It appears that most Muslims prefer the first of these options.

Endnotes

[1] The Ka'aba is the object of the pilgrimage to Mecca that all Muslims are obliged to make once in a lifetime.

[2] This section and the one following it are based on John L. Esposito, *Islam: The Straight Path*, New York: Oxford, 1988, pp. 68-95 and Albert Hourani, *A History of the Arab Peoples*, Cambridge, Mass.: Harvard 1991, pp. 59-72, 147-52.

[3] All references from the Quran will be listed by chapter and verse; they are taken from the Penguin 4th edition, N. J. Dawood translator, New York, 1974.

[4] Esposito, p. 83.

[5] This section is based on Hourani, pp. 181-6.

⁶ This section is based on Charles Issawi, "The Adaption of Islam to Contemporary Economic Realities," *The Islamic Impact*, Yvonne Haddad, Byron Haines and Ellison Findly editors, Syracuse: Syracuse University, 1984, pp. 27-46; Muhammed Nayatullah Siddiqi, "An Islamic Approach to Economics," *Islam: Source and Purpose of Knowledge*, Herndon, Va.: Int. Inst. 1988, pp. 165-74; Mustafa Mahmud, "Islam vs. Marxism and Capitalism," *Islam in Transition: Muslim Perspectives*, John Donohue and John Esposito editors, New York: Harper & Row, 1982, pp. 155-9; Sayyid Qutb, "Social Justice in Islam," *Ibid.*, pp. 126-8; Muhammed Zafrulla Khan, *Islam: Its Meaning for Modern Man*, New York: Oxford 1962, pp. 150-7; Patrick Bannerman, *Islam in Perspective*, London: Routledge 1988, pp. 96-108; Ziauddin Sardar, *Islamic Futures: The Shape of Ideas to Come*, London: Mansell, 1985, pp. 198-217.

⁷ Bannerman, p. 108.

⁸ Sardar, p. 199.

⁹ Ayatullah Mahmud Taliqani, "The Characteristics of Islamic Economics," *Islam in Transition*, p. 214.

¹⁰ Qutb, p. 127.

¹¹This section is based on Jane Smith, "The Experience of Muslim Women," *The Islamic Impact*, pp. 89-112; R.W.J. Austin, "Islam and the Feminine," *Islam in the Modern World*, Denis MacEoin and Ahmed al-Shahi editors, New York: St. Martin's, 1983, pp. 36-48; Lisa Beyer, "Life Behind the Veil," *Time Special Issue: Women*, Fall 1990, p. 37; Esposito, pp. 95-103, 186-92.

¹² Smith, p. 92.

¹³ Esposito, p. 97-8.

¹⁴ Maulana Muhammed Ali, *A Manual of Hadith*, Lahore: Curzon Press, 1944, p. 284.

¹⁵ Beyer, p. 37.

¹⁶ Smith, p. 109.

¹⁷ This section is based on Khan, pp. 170-83; Bannerman, pp. 83-95 and Majid Khadduri, *The Islamic Conception of Justice*, Baltimore: Johns Hopkins, 1984, pp. 161-73.

¹⁸ Khadduri, pp. 163-4.

¹⁹ *Ibid.*, p. 169.

Suggestions for Further Reading

Catholicism

Dorr, Donal. *Option for the Poor: A Hundred Years of Vatican Social Teaching.* Maryknoll, N.Y.: Orbis, 1983.

Schultheis, Michael J., Edward P. DeBerri, and Peter J. Henriot. *Our Best Kept Secret: The Rich Heritage of Catholic Social Teaching.* Washington, D.C.: Center of Concern, 1987.

Gremillion, Joseph, editor. *The Gospel of Peace and Justice: Catholic Social Teaching Since Pope John.* Maryknoll, N.Y.: Orbis, 1976.

McBrien, Richard P. *Catholicism: Study Edition.* Minneapolis: Winston, 1981.

The Catholic Bishops' Pastoral Letters

National Conference of Catholic Bishops. *The Challenge of Peace: God's Promise and Our Response.* Washington, D.C.: United States Catholic Conference, 1983.

_____. *Economic Justice for All: Pastoral Letter on Catholic Social Teaching and the U.S. Economy.* Washington, D.C.: United States Catholic Conference, 1986.

_____. *Partners in the Mystery of Redemption: A Pastoral Response to Women's Concerns for Church and Society. Origins,* Vol. 17, No. 45 (April 21, 1988), pp. 757-788.

Protestantism

Brown, Robert McAfee. *The Spirit of Protestantism.* New York: Oxford, 1965.

Forrell, George W. *The Protestant Faith.* Englewood Cliffs, N. J.: Prentice-Hall, 1960.

Marty, Martin. *Protestantism.* New York: Holt, Rinehart and Winston, 1972.

Niebuhr, H. Richard. *Christ and Culture.* New York: Harper & Brothers, 1951.

Rauschenbusch, Walter. *A Theory of the Social Gospel.* Nashville: Parthenon Press, 1917, reprinted 1978.

Judaism

Bernfeld, Simon. *The Foundations of Jewish Ethics.* Armin Hajman Koller, translator. New York: KTAV Publishing House, 1968.

Hertzberg, Arthur. *Judaism.* New York: George Braziller, 1962.

Konvitz, Milton R., editor. *Judaism and Human Rights.* New York: W. W. Norton, 1972.

Steinberg, Milton. *Basic Judaism.* New York: Harcourt, Brace & World, 1947.

Islam

Lippman, Thomas W. *Understanding Islam: An Introduction to the Muslim World.* New York: Mentor, 1990.

Esposito, John L. *Islam: The Straight Path.* New York: Oxford, 1988.

Hourani, Albert. *A History of the Arab Peoples.* Cambridge, Mass.: Harvard, 1991.

Khadduri, Majid. *The Islamic Conception of Justice.* Baltimore: John Hopkins, 1984.

Profiles of Contributors

James J. Horgan (Ph. D., Saint Louis University) is professor of history and chairs the division of social science at Saint Leo College. He is the author of *City of Flight* (1984) and *Pioneer College* (1990), co-editor of *The Reagan Years* (1988), and has compiled two collections of letters on the origins of the Catholic Colony of San Antonio, Florida. He has published in such journals as *Southern Exposure, The Florida Historical Society Report,* and *Educational Record.* He has served as national director of research for the United Farm Workers Union. In 1968 he received a distinguished service award from the Florida NAACP and in 1986 a citation from the Carnegie Foundation for the Advancement of Teaching.

Lucy Fuchs (Ph. D., University of South Florida) is associate professor of education at Saint Leo College. She is the author of *Ways With Words* (1988), *Forgiveness* (1990), and *Gifts and Giving* (1991), as well as two monographs on reading and four novels. She has published more than 150 articles in such journals as *The Reading Teacher, Learning, Florida Educational Computing Quarterly, Curriculum Review, Journal of Educational Studies, Catholic Life,* and *Religion Teacher's Journal.* She is a frequent speaker at workshops and conferences. She serves on a parish educational mission team for the Dominican Republic and in 1980 received an award from the International Reading Association.

Jeanine Jacob (M. A., Fordham University) is state editor of *The Florida Catholic,* the statewide newspaper of the Catholic dioceses of Florida. She is former director of communications for Saint Leo College. She has published in such journals as *Columbia, Maryknoll, Catholic*

Digest, and *Jewish Floridian.* She is a member of Florida Press Women and serves on the national communications committee of the United States Catholic Conference. She received a writing award from *Atlantic Monthly,* as well as a news writing citation from the Catholic Press Association in 1982 and a 1986 award from the United States Catholic Conference.

Bernard S. Parker (Ph. D., Tulane University) is president of Saint Mary of the Plains College in Dodge City, Kansas. He was formerly professor of philosophy and vice president for academic affairs at Saint Leo College. He is the co-editor of *The Examination of Belief* (1984) and has written articles on philosophy and on educational issues for such publications as *Educational Record* and the *Southern Quarterly.* He was a 1964-1965 Woodrow Wilson Fellow at the University of Chicago, and in 1984-1985 a fellow of the American Council on Education.

Joseph A. Cernik (Ph. D., New York University) is associate professor of public administration and international business at Lindenwood College in St. Charles, Missouri, and former political science faculty member at Saint Leo College, where he organized the Saint Leo College Press. He co-edited and contributed a chapter on nuclear policy to *The Reagan Years.* He has received fellowships for advanced study at the U. S. Military Academy and the University of Miami. He has published in the fields of Soviet-American relations, nuclear strategy, and the Civil War in Florida.

S. Mary David Hydro, O.S.B. (Master of Christian Spirituality, Creighton University) is a member of the Sisters of Saint Benedict of Florida at Holy Name Priory in Saint Leo, where she is formation directress. She is also adjunct professor of theology at Saint Leo College. She is a member of Pax Christi and a former state council member of its Florida chapter.

Charles Lewis Fisk Jr. (M.A., Duke University) is an associate professor of economics at Saint Leo College, where he specializes in economic thought and U.S. economic history. He was a member of Phi Beta Kappa at the University of Florida. He contributed a chapter on economic policy to *The Reagan Years*, and has published other articles on economic issues. He is also a sports columnist for the *Pasco Today*.

Jude Michael Ryan (M. A., University of South Florida) is a member of the English department at Polk Community College in Lakeland, Florida and a 1975 graduate of Saint Leo College. He has been a guest columnist for the *St. Petersburg Times*.

Christine Cherry Cernik (M. D., Rush Medical College) is a practicing obstetrician-gynecologist in St. Louis, Missouri. She has published in the *St. Louis Post-Dispatch* and *Media Profiles*. She has also lectured on women and AIDS, women in sports, and other issues of women's health. In addition, she has appeared on *Health Matters*, a televised health education program, and is a frequent St. Louis television commentator on health issues.

David T. Borton (Master of Theological Studies, Trinity Lutheran Seminary) writes a monthly column on social justice titled "The Gospel Calls" for the Episcopal Diocese of Southwest Florida. He has been a refugee resettlement worker with the Lutheran Ministries of Florida and is now manager for employee relations at Tampa General Hospital.

Kathleen Kosuda (M. L. S., State University of New York at Albany) is library director at Saint Leo College.

She is a member of the board of the Tampa Bay Library Consortium and serves on a national committee of the American Library Association. She has published articles in *Educator's Update* and *Catholic Library World.*

John J. McTague (Ph. D., State University of New York at Buffalo) is a professor of history at Saint Leo College, where he also coordinates the college's international studies program. He is the author of *British Policy in Palestine, 1917-1922* (1983) and contributed an article on U.S.-Israeli relations to *The Reagan Years.* He has published articles in such journals as *Jewish Social Studies* and the *Journal of Palestine Studies.* His book reviews have appeared in the *American Historical Review, Perspective,* and the *Tampa Tribune.* He is book review editor for *Middle East Research Analysis,* as well as a sports columnist for *Pasco Today.*

This is the fifth book published by the Saint Leo College Press, following *The Reagan Years: Perspectives and Assessments* (1988), *Pioneer College: The Centennial History of Saint Leo College, Saint Leo Abbey, and Holy Name Priory* (1990), *Divided We Fall: Essays on Confederate Nation-Building* (1991), and *Rivers to Skyscrapers: Ethics in Modern American Literature* (1991).

Saint Leo College is a Catholic, four-year liberal arts college, chartered by the Order of St. Benedict of Florida in 1889. Its main campus is located in Pasco County, 25 miles north of Tampa. The college has extension centers throughout Florida and operates degree programs on military bases throughout the southeastern United States.